Marketing Your School

*Stand out from the crowd by meeting the
needs of your parents and your community*

Simon Hepburn

ABOUT THIS BOOK

'Marketing Your School' shows how learning from marketing practices widely used in other industries can help all schools to form closer relationships with parents and the wider school community, increase recruitment and make sure that their school is both innovative and well-known for innovation.

The book is a guide to marketing for all those involved in running schools in the UK - head teachers and other SLT members, Governors, those responsible for marketing schools, and those running chains of academies and free schools. It covers both the state and independent sectors and all types of school from large secondary schools to small primary and special schools.

The book starts by considering how marketing fits with the overall school strategy, how to find and listen to local communities, and how a school can create a clear and consistent message. It explains how to set a marketing budget, create a strategic marketing plan, develop a wide range of evidence to support your messaging, and to evaluate success.

It then focuses on the practical challenges of marketing - including ideas to enhance student and staff recruitment, improve Open Days, achieve more media coverage and make the best use of the latest social media platforms to engage stakeholders.

Specialist contributors explain how to help introduce marketing to a school, create a design that communicates your school's unique message, use the best IT software to manage contacts and use the latest technology to revolutionise your traditional school newsletter.

Marketing never stands still though and this book will begin to date from the moment it is published. To keep up with the latest ideas, please visit marketingadviceforschools.com, the 'website of the book', and sign up for your free monthly newsletter or follow @mktadvice4schls on Twitter.

ACKNOWLEDGEMENTS

I would like to thank the school marketing community both in the UK and USA for their help and advice over the past two years. I'm very grateful to marketing experts Tim Latham, Nic Eversett, Sarah Clarke, and Helen West for allowing me to use their articles in this book (the EXPERT ADVICE sections) and to Helen again for the illustrations.

I'd also like to thank them and Brendan Schneider, Liza Fisher Norman, Jonathan Fingerhut, Anne Nicholls, Mark Woodward, Randy Vaughan, Ben Gibbs and Julia Acklam for sharing their ideas on school marketing in person or online.

It has also been a privilege to learn from schools who are marketing well. I'd particularly like to thank the schools featured in the book – Sewickley Academy, Bablake School, Whitefields Primary School, Langdale Primary School, St Bede's College and St Mary's, Levenshulme – and all those who have shared their ideas via the Twitter feed Good News from Schools (@goodnews_schls).

Finally, many thanks to David Brookman for extensive advice and proofing, Rachael for all her support, ideas and proofreading – and to Ivo for being Ivo.

Simon Hepburn

Timperley, August 2014

CONTENTS

CHAPTER ONE: INTRODUCTION – THE MARKETING CYCLE

a) What is marketing?

A common view is that marketing is the same as advertising, but advertising is only a small part of the discipline. Marketing is the process by which an organisation identifies its customers, finds out about their needs, changes its offering in response and then communicates the offering to develop and grow the organisation. This book uses the **Marketing Cycle** model below to explain and explore marketing.

Market Research – Marketing starts by talking to current and potential parents, finding out about competing schools, looking for external developments that affect your school, making links with other stakeholders (organisations and people who can help you succeed) and evaluating different ways of communicating to all stakeholders.

Meeting Market Needs – Once your school know what its stakeholders want, it needs to make sure these needs are met. For example, parents may want new subjects, better transport links or innovative ways of teaching their children.

Message and Brand Development – A school should then develop a small number of key messages and a consistent style of design and writing to ensure consistency when communicating why it is different.

Gathering Evidence – A school needs to find the stories that support these key messages, working with current and former students, parents and teachers. This can include conducting research and creating experts on educational issues. The stories should be used again and again for maximum impact.

Using Mass Media – A school must make best use of the many different ways of communicating with parents and other stakeholders including its website; advertising; media relations; social media; direct mail and email; events; exhibitions; publications and face-to-face meetings.

Relationship Management - Anyone who expresses an interest in the school needs to be identified and then communicated with on a regular basis to ensure they choose your school (or support it in other ways for other stakeholders).

PLUS… Marketing Management – as well as planning the process above at the start, good marketing requires careful planning and reflection to drive improvement.

b) Why do schools need to take marketing seriously?

In business and higher education, organisations spend much of their time and effort (and up to 10% of their turnover) on marketing. They research markets, spend huge amounts of time and effort on targeting customers through advertising and manage huge customer databases. By contrast, marketing is a much lower priority in many schools.

This is probably because until recently this did not matter. Some schools were good at marketing but for many the concept was not very important. During the economic boom between 1998 and 2008 many private schools had long waiting lists and competition between state schools was limited.

Now due to economic and political realities, to succeed all schools must do more than 'a good job in the classroom'. They need to compete for students and the competition is growing - academies, free schools, chains of independent schools and so on.

With all schools receiving their income on a per student basis, recruiting just one extra student should bring at least £20,000 extra to the school over their time at the school (and this number typically trebles for private schools).

Even those schools that are 'full' now must show that they are listening to and responding to parents – with OFSTED for example launching 'Parent View' online surveys in 2011[1] - as well as ensuring that their reputation is strong enough to survive changes in their market.

---

[1] parentview.ofsted.gov.uk

However, compared to other sectors, there is relatively little marketing expertise in the sector. The vast majority of school leaders have spent almost all of their career as teachers. They might acquire knowledge of finance and people management via the NPQH or time as a Deputy Head, but few learn marketing skills on the way to the top. Compare this with the newly appointed Managing Director of a similar sized multi-million pound business. They often have an MBA or equivalent qualification that has significant marketing content, as well as a dedicated marketing team.

The result is that schools have many hard working senior staff who are good at placing adverts in local papers, running open days and selling the school to individual parents, but have little knowledge of the wider aspects of marketing. This book will help with immediate pupil recruitment, but also outlines a wider, strategic approach to marketing in schools - identifying potential customers early whilst creating a brand and key messages that attract and maintaining a culture of continual communication and improvement.

This approach has many positive benefits as well as improving recruitment. A marketing focus will improve the service offered by schools and make it easier to respond to the needs of parents and students. A school will be able to align staff behind a set of core values more easily if it can show them in practice. It will find interesting stories from all parts of the organisation and develop the confidence and talents of students and staff. Internal communication becomes easier. A school might end up with a new school newspaper or TV station!

On the other hand, schools that don't listen to and respond to customers can suddenly find themselves with a poor reputation compared to others. This can lead to falling rolls and a negative spiral into trouble!

c) What if a school's Head doesn't 'believe' in marketing?

EXPERT ADVICE from marketingadviceforschools.com

By Nic Eversett, school marketer and primary school teacher

1. Don't call it marketing

Although marketing is becoming more accepted, many Head Teachers remain uneasy about it because they believe it is something used by profit making companies. As a result, they are resistant to the idea of marketing. So, consider presenting your proposals as promotional activities or ideas for raising the school's profile – or as a specific response to a need such as poor recruitment.

2. It's about the parents

In most cases Heads will take up your offer of marketing support because they need to improve communications with parents, both current and future. Considering the regularity of contact between parents and school, far higher than in most businesses, schools often know little about their parent 'customers'. Help them to see that good communication with parents needs to be relevant, regular and reciprocal.

3. Start with practical ideas

Because marketing will be perceived as a fringe activity, there will be little opportunity to explain complex marketing ideas. I recommend that you should focus on initially on straightforward ways to improve schools communication. Typical areas will be:

- Revamping the school prospectus or other recruitment literature.
- Improving the school's web presence. Most schools have a web site but they are often poorly constructed and maintained.

Offering a more effective delivery of existing communications, such as email newsletters. Schools are looking for ways to communicate more, better and cheaper.

4. Remember every school is different

This may seems an obvious point but schools have a very strong image of themselves and see themselves as totally unique. Therefore in order to be taken seriously by school heads, the ability to present the 'unique ethos' of the school will be an essential, yet unspoken aim.

5. Make sure you link different marketing activities

Schools often don't have the resources to manage several organisations to provide parts of their communications needs. For many schools each individual element is often not a significant project. Schools often find it difficult to present materials consistently.

6. Be bright, be brief, be gone

Inevitably, you will be competing with the Head's day to day concerns. Therefore everything you say or write needs to be very concise and focused on clear benefits. Don't forget the Head may have to explain what you have told them to the Governors, so it is important the benefits are easily and immediately grasped.

d) How marketing helped Sewickley Academy

CASE STUDY from marketingadviceforschools.com

Brendan Schneider had not been long in post as *Director of Admissions at Sewickley Academy in Pittsburgh, USA*, when the economic downturn hit - leading the school on a journey to reinvent marketing for a digital age and Brendan on a larger mission to re-educate school marketers!

He takes up the story,

"When the U.S. Stock Market crashed in October 2008 we almost immediately noticed an impact on our recruiting. Our interest indicators; inquiries, applications, and visits, began to decline and trended downward all school year. As a result we immediately began to brainstorm ideas to help stop the downward trend. Our first efforts though led us to outbound ('traditional') marketing techniques we hadn't tried in the past including the use of billboards, advertising in Pittsburgh International Airport, and hyper-targeting our direct mail campaigns. The problem was that all of those efforts did not help to increase our inquiries, applications, and visits.

"We next turned to social media and launched our Facebook page and Twitter account. We thought that social media would solve our problems. We were wrong! Social media by itself did not help to solve the problem - while we increased our number of likes and followers our inquiries, applications, and visits didn't increase.

"While we were trying these other techniques I picked up a copy of *Inbound Marketing: Get Found Using Google, Social Media, and Blogs* by Brian Halligan and Dharmesh Shah. I was hooked - I knew we had to try inbound marketing. I purchased a copy of the book for my Head of School to read and he was willing to give inbound marketing a try".

13

Inbound marketing is all about creating content that will encourage people to learn about your school, as well as making sure that potential parents and students can find it by ensuring the content is easily found on search engines and shared on social media. It reflects the fact that most consumers use technology to find solutions to their problems.

For a good example of how inbound marketing works itself, try Googling 'private schools in Pittsburgh'. Not only do you quickly reach Sewickley's website, but you also find yourself drawn to a range of interesting blogs - written by staff, parents, alumni and students. You're also encouraged to sign up to new blog posts or to share them with your social media contacts. The Academy's YouTube site has a similar feel - rather than a formal admissions video, there's a real insight into the school - and it's interesting to see that the most shared videos show students talking about their own views of the Academy.

So, what has been the impact of this change? Brendan has some good news to report – "Last school year our inquiries, applications, and visits all saw great increases and I equate that positive difference to inbound marketing."

What advice would Brendan give to other schools looking to improve their marketing?

"I'm still surprised that schools have been so slow to even experiment with inbound marketing. Simply putting your social media icons in non-digital marketing is not enough. The schools that are doing it well try to engage their audience in the non-digital space with a call-to-action guiding them to social media - hopefully using a tracking URL' - monitoring what works is a key part of inbound marketing.

Given the evolving nature of technology, it's not surprising that neither Brendan nor Sewickley are not standing still. When asked what he's

most excited about, Brendan replies,

'Great question! I'm constantly reading and participating on social media channels looking for new ideas and how I can apply them to marketing my school. I think a school should ask themselves three questions before launching a new social media channel:

1. Is their current or prospective audience on the channel?

2. What are the goals of using the channel and how will they measure their efforts?

3. Finally, who will create content and manage the channel?

A school must answer these questions before they launch then make a determination if it's smart for their school to participate in the channel. We conducted webinars last year and just released the first eBook for our school. I'm already thinking about our next eBook as well as conducting Facebook contests among some other ideas. You'll have to follow my school on social media (@Sewickley on Twitter) to see what we have planned."

[Inbound marketing is the approach that is explored in chapters 6-8 of this book – once you're clear about your market and what makes your school stand out!]

Sewickley Academy, Pittsburgh

15

CHAPTER TWO: MANAGING MARKETING (PART I: SETTING UP)

This chapter covers the management decisions that need to be taken before a marketing programme is put in place. Chapter 9 picks up the management theme at the end of the process with reflection and evaluation of marketing.

a) Creating a strategic marketing plan

Marketing success must be linked to organisational goals such as the attraction and retention of students. The best way to do this is to create a strategic marketing plan as an integral part of the wider development plan of the school.

The strategic marketing plan needs to set out what the school's organisational objectives are, link these to marketing objectives and outline how they can be met.

An individual school's organisational objectives will determine where its marketing priorities lie – for some schools the most important task is to work out the key messages to communicate (Chapter 5), while for others it is creating a sensible communications plan covering three or four areas of the marketing mix (Chapter 7). It often helps to think of organisational and marketing objectives as either short, medium or long term – for a school a short term would be within the next month, medium term in the next school year and long term over a period of 2 or more years.

Marketing objectives need if possible to be SMART - specific, measurable, achievable, realistic and time-bound – although it is important not to focus too tightly on specific numbers especially in the first year of a marketing programme. As an example, if a new 'free' primary school or school Sixth Form needs to have an intake of 60 students, the most important marketing objectives could be to clearly define the 'brand' of the school, make contact with 600 local parents, have 300 visit the school and achieve 120 applications.

In an established secondary school that is looking to grow its reputation (but has no immediate recruitment issues), the marketing objectives could be to clearly identify and communicate what makes the school distinctive and aim to make 80% of current parents and 50% of those in feeder schools aware of these differentials – assessing progress through market research.

The marketing strategy then needs to clearly show the actions that will be taken over time to achieve these objectives. In all cases it is important to assign a budget and agree responsibility for each actions. The actions need also need a fixed deadline that works with the wider school calendar (with a particular focus on key admission dates).

Finally, the strategic marketing plan should state what evaluation will take place, when and by whom. It is vital that marketing objectives are measured regularly and evaluation takes place on a regular basis (at least monthly) during the year so that major deviations from the initial plan can be identified and action taken.

Excerpt from a sample strategic marketing plan (with the budget, timing, targets and responsibility columns removed)

Organisational Objective	Marketing Objective	Actions
Attract 10% more pupils to Year 7	Increase awareness of school	Press ad package in local newspaper
		Online ad package in local newspaper
		Press ads in relevant local magazines
		Create and print Posters/flyers/postcards
		Banners / posters in key locations
		End of Term College Newsletter printed & distributed
	PR campaign focused on target parents	5 PR stories in key titles (online/offline)
		Prospectus with real stories
		Twitter feed with regular updates
		Monthly electronic newsletter
	Create relationships with all feeder schools	Identify all feeder schools (current & potential)
		Nominate staff member to be Primary Link
		Primary Link to contact all schools
		Primary Link to visit 50% of schools
		Postcards/flyers/giveaways to all feeder schools (when Link person visits)
		Open Day dates agreed
		Taster days for Years 5 and 6 in Easter/Whit holidays
		In-school events inviting potential parents & pupils (e.g. Drama / arts / music / sports)

b) Setting a marketing budget

Schools already spend a lot of money on marketing activities - creating and running advertising, producing prospectuses, creating display material and running open days for a start. Putting these costs together into a marketing budget allows the marketing team to reduce the costs of most activities as well as eliminating duplication of effort and other unproductive work. This will allow money to be reallocated into areas such as customer relationship management databases and market research.

A standard marketing budget sets out proposed spend per month across the range of organisational and marketing objectives, divided into the various tactical activities used. Spend per month will vary for discretionary activities such as advertising (high around key admission deadlines, lower in the summer), while other costs (salaries, subscriptions, media relations consultancy) tend to be fixed. While some flexibility between months should be expected, it is very important to maintain a contingency reserve to help with specific recruitment or other business-critical needs.

Sample marketing budget for a typical secondary school:

Activity	Jan	Feb	Mar
Salaries	3,000	3,000	3,000
Subscriptions	100	100	100
Print advertising	5,000	2,000	2,000
Google AdWords	1,000	1,000	1,000
Publications	0	500	500
Direct Mail	100	2,000	2,000
Website	0	0	1,000
Media Relations	500	500	500
Contingency	500	500	500
TOTAL	10,200	10,600	10,600

c) Making the most of the marketing budget

Schools don't have a lot of room to manoeuvre in their marketing budgets. However, there are some ways to make the most of the available money:

1. Always ask for discounts.

Remember that any price is simply an indication of what someone wants to sell their product for, not what it actually costs them - and suppliers do deals all the time.

2. Buy in bulk.

Printing is a great example where significant savings can be made by ordering as much as possible. One example is the cost of a school prospectus - rather than short runs of a new document every year, leave out year-specific information such as exam results, order glossy folders and then print loose-leaf information to update the document for a second year and see a reduction of 50% in printing costs.

3. Book well in advance.

Committing to advertising in a publication early should save at least 10% (and in some cases a lot more).

4. Alternatively, book at the last minute.

Waiting until close to publication deadline can see bigger discounts (75% is possible) if you're the only bidder for the space. This often happens with new publications.

5. Ask for extras to maximise your spend.

Ask a publication ask if they'll promote your school on their website, upgrade the placing of the advert or give your school copies of the publication to distribute.

6. Evaluate marketing spend and cut out what doesn't work.

Don't just 'roll over' every publication you advertise in - make it a rule to move at least 10% of advertising spend each year.

7. Plan ahead to share and reuse content.

Make sure that the design of adverts is not changed too often (leading to expensive design costs) and that same stories are reused throughout your advertising, social media and media relations programmes.

8. Create a flexible, reusable design.

Ask your designer to create illustration, borders and other elements that can be used across a range of publications.

9. Look for free ways to share news.

Remember to ask all your stakeholders to help. Schools will often find parents, governors and teachers who can offer advertising in shops, businesses and community and religious organisations.

10. Look online for savings.

You can save on stock photography, printing, web design, email newsletters and even copy writing online. But be careful not to use artwork without permission.

One major don't...

Skimp on the bits where you really need help. There are some areas (photography of your school, design, video, advertising copywriting) that really make a difference in marketing. You may have experts at these within your school (check they are really experts by giving them a small task first!), but it is worth spending money in these areas to get your messages clearly communicated.

d) Who should lead marketing in a school?

Given that the role of marketing includes helping to set the strategic direction of a school as well as advising on how changes are communicated to key stakeholders, marketing clearly needs to be represented on the Senior Leadership Team of a school. Given the importance of reputation to school success, there is also a clear need for marketing activity to be discussed regularly with the school Governing Body.

Some aspects of marketing, particularly media relations and social media management (see chapter 7) also require a lot of flexibility during the working day, which is not possible for teachers who have a full teaching load. In addition, while marketing can be seen as a 'creative' function, in a small team or individual it is vital that this is matched with strong attention to detail.

Given these restrictions here are the options for a school creating or updating their marketing function:

1. **A marketing team**. For very large state schools, all independent schools and small academy chains, a marketing department should be set up led by a full time **Marketing Director** who sits on the Senior Management Team. As well as marketing they could also be responsible for Alumni Development, Admissions and/or other support functions.

The Marketing Director should be supported by at least a Marketing Assistant so that someone is available at all times to deal with enquiries from prospective parents and from the media. If the school is planning significant advertising or several events, one or more additional marketing staff or teachers with specific expertise could take responsibility for these areas. In this model, qualified marketing professionals with experience outside of education and perhaps CIM (Chartered Institute of Marketing) qualifications could be used, provided they were sensitive to the challenges of working in a school.

As academies grow in size, the preferred model for large chains seems to be for a central marketing function with regional representatives looking after and feeding back information from across the country. This has the advantage of ensuring a consistent brand while allowing different parts of the country to develop different messages and stories to meet the needs of what can be wildly different audiences.

2. Medium sized secondary schools and sixth form colleges should consider employing **a professional Marketing Manager** reporting to the Business Manager or Head. This has the advantage of fitting into an existing structure while providing continual focus on marketing. It will be important to choose an individual who is self-starting and who can understand the unique challenges of working in a school - perhaps someone who has had teaching experience themselves.

3. An alternative for smaller schools would be to give responsibility to the **Business Manager or to a senior teacher who sits on the Senior Leadership Team**. It is important that they receive training in advance of starting work in this area, and are supported in continuing this through their appointment. In addition, to ensure availability, they should be supported by at least one trained marketing professional - either a recent graduate **Marketing Executive** or a **Marketing Assistant**. These could also take on other administrative tasks in other areas of the school, but would provide a consistent point of contact with the wider world.

4. Very small schools have no real alternative than to give responsibility to **one teacher (or the head teacher)**. However, it is difficult to see how a full time teacher could satisfactorily manage media relations or handle enquiries from potential customers in a timely fashion in all but the smallest schools. In these cases, an administrator in the school should be trained to support the marketing teacher or an external agency brought in to provide support.

5. One final approach is using volunteers to undertake strategic or ongoing marketing tasks. This however is problematic for the reasons below.

a) Volunteers invariably have other calls on their time – whether paid work or caring roles – and it is unlikely that volunteers will be able to devote the same amount of time to marketing a school over a long time period.

b) Volunteers can have conflicts of interest – they may take on a volunteer role and then get a paid job with a competitor for example or work for an organisation that pitches for business with your school.

c) Volunteers cannot be held to specific targets – companies or people you hire can be performance managed and held to account. It is difficult to tell a volunteer to work harder!

d) Using volunteers stops you getting the best people for the job – a school would not take on a volunteer to teach a class or to do the school accounts or plumbing. Marketing is an important part of a school's future and you need the best people to do the job.

A better solution for schools who have parents or governors with marketing experience is to use them to help recruit and assess the performance of marketing experts, not to replace them.

e) Recruiting school marketers

Schools marketing is an expanding sector – the number of jobs shared on marketingadviceforschools.com has doubled in the past two years for example. In an expanding market the easiest recruitment method – finding someone from a similar background - is more difficult. So, what are your options?

Hiring a marketer from another industry seems the obvious option. But there are problems with this approach - do senior marketers from industry know education, do they know the challenges of working in a school, do they even have the breadth of knowledge of all the marketing techniques needed?

Perhaps it's better to train up a teacher or senior manager? The problems here are actually quite similar - as a school is a small place, there is a lot to learn and little support from other marketers. While training is widely available, it takes time and money to gain CIM qualifications for example.

A better approach is to look at the three most practically important skills and attributes for a school marketer:

1. A wide range of marketing experience: Consider hiring from small companies where a marketer will have experience of all aspects of marketing from PR to advertising, direct mail to website design.

2. A knowledge of and interest in education: A school is very different from any other workplace. It is essential to understand and appreciate the roles of teachers and other staff in a school.

3. A proactive approach: In a very small team a marketer needs to be able to make progress themselves towards goals without waiting for approval.

f) The cost of school marketers

School marketing salaries vary tremendously. At the top end, Marketing Directors of top independent schools can earn £70,000 or more (especially if they also have responsibility for Development or Admissions). Marketing Manager positions were being advertised in the range £30-40,000 in July 2014, while Marketing Executives were earning from £20-25,000. Many state schools also advertise for part-time and/or term-time positions at lower salaries that focus on creative tasks, while administrators in the school take enquiries. There is significant regional variation in salaries, with the South and South East paying the top end of the range above and the North of England the lower end.

These figures (from jobs mentioned on marketingadvicefor-schools.com) fit well with other industry research. The 2012 Marketing Week salary survey[2] found that Marketing Directors in Charities (perhaps the best comparator - probably with 10 years plus experience and an MBA) earned around £50,000 while a Marketing Manager (graduate with 5 years' experience and a Chartered Institute of Marketing (CIM) Diploma) would typically earn £39,000 and a Marketing Executive (graduate with a CIM Advanced Certificate) would expect to earn around £25,000. A Marketing Assistant role would pay from £15,000 depending on the marketing qualifications of the individual.

Salaries will rise over time, especially when the economy improves – it is always worth checking recent adverts or asking recruitment consultancies to get a sense of the current salary level.

When calculating the total costs of a marketer it is important to add in wider employment costs such as National Insurance and pension contributions as well as their office running costs. A 2-person

---

[2] www.marketingweek.co.uk/the-marketing-week/ball-and-hoolahan-salary-survey-2012/3033165.article

marketing department could cost over £90,000 pa – although for schools with pupil shortages this would be covered by recruiting as few as 5 extra state (or 2 private) pupils per year, even assuming the full-time team were not able to make savings on existing marketing spend.

g) Using marketing consultants – a useful alternative

External consultants can be very useful to schools. They offer expert advice, can take over any and all aspects of a school's marketing function and can provide cover through the full teaching day, if teachers are used as marketers. On the other hand, they can be expensive. Here are some tips for getting the most from consultants.

1. Use them where they add the most value.

Signing an ongoing contract with a consultant can prove expensive, especially if they duplicate resources you have internally. It is however always worth paying for an expert if the specific expertise is not available in-house. Here are four of the best times to use consultants:

-   To help set up marketing in a school, in particular when a new school opens or changes status but also when a school moves to a new IT system or starts actively marketing itself for the first time.
-   To perform one off specialist tasks such as marketing research, setting up a website or creating a design for the school's brand – tasks that perhaps take place once every one or two years.
-   To take on a specialist role, such as media relations or direct mail fulfilment, where they will work for a number of different clients at the same time and reduce the cost to an individual school.
-   For expert advice when specific issues arise (for example external communication in the aftermath of a crisis).

2. Find a specialist who understands schools.

Working in a school is very different from other workplaces and agencies that don't understand the specific challenges of the sector will struggle to understand a brief and come up with the right solution.

3. Talk to at least three consultancies and take up references

Don't make decisions too quickly – it can be very tempting to choose a consultancy that has done similar work for a couple of local schools or one that is recommended by a personal contact, but it is important to do some research and talk to a number of consultancies. The best ones will also help you frame your needs and reduce costs as they look for a long-term relationship.

4. Set clear objectives

Be very clear about what you want the consultancy to achieve and link these objectives to your development plan and marketing strategy.

5. Be very clear about who is doing the work & what is being charged for

One of the biggest criticisms of consultancies is that they will make great promises and use their most experienced and senior staff to win business, but once signed up a client only ever sees and hears from junior staff. In a similar way be careful that all expenses are in the initial contract. As mentioned in the budgeting section later in this chapter it is a good idea to keep a contingency fund of around 10% so a small amount of useful additional work can be paid for. Consultancies usually charge by project or by day. Expect to pay from £300 to over £1,000 per day depending on the seniority of the person working on your account.

6. Keep talking to them

Communication is vital, especially at the start of their work. A consultancy will need to meet with a wide range of people in the school and create channels so they can hear about all the great things schools are doing – make sure time and budget is allowed for this. The school also needs to know of any problems with any aspect of the marketing programme very early.

h) Engaging staff, parents and students

For a successful marketing campaign to work, staff, parents and current students must be engaged. All are highly influential in the process of choosing schools and can be powerful advocates if they are given the right materials and stories. The key to this is to invite them to contribute time, stories and marketing ideas, to continually communicate progress and successes to them, and to enable them to pass on key marketing messages to the wider community.

Parents often have experience of one or more aspects of marketing and can help in many areas. Indeed Parent Teacher Associations already do a lot of marketing. Parents are generally unsurprised that a school wants to talk about its activities and advertise – they are told that they are consumers of education and expect to be given information to allow them to make choices. Setting up a parent marketing forum allows them to volunteer their expertise. Members of staff may already know parents who they would like to invite to this.

Students also are pleased to have their achievements highlighted and will enjoy the opportunities to write news stories and direct video if you set up a student news team (as suggested in chapter 6). It is important to check with students and their parents before directly involving them in marketing - some aspects of safeguarding are relevant and are also covered in chapter 6. Marketing plans and successes can also be shared with School Councils and similar representative bodies.

Many teachers will also happily engage with marketing and should be invited to help whenever possible (a staff marketing committee is always a good idea), although some will see marketing as something that has the potential to get in the way of their main role, teaching. Regular updates on marketing progress and targeted rather than general requests for help are important. The marketing leader in the school should also attend department or faculty meetings on a regular basis to explain their role and current projects.

i) Managing Time, Setting Priorities and Working with Teachers

When starting a marketing programme there is a lot to get to grips with, especially if the person or team responsible are new to a school or to education and also need to settle in to the organisation. At the same time there will be pressure to show the impact of the marketing focus quickly.

The best way to manage this dilemma is to plan for a few short-term 'quick wins' while also setting up the processes that will lead to long term success.

For example, it would be sensible to develop a number of news stories and case studies to freshen up existing marketing materials and achieve improved media coverage. This would enable links to be made with a number of teachers and students and create a positive impression of marketing across the school. While this is happening, the parent, staff and student research that will lead to longer-term changes can be set up.

When asking teachers or parents for help it is important to be aware that they have other priorities – to help overcome this, make sure that there are clear guidelines and examples wherever possible.

Chapter Checklist...

- ☐ Is there a realistic central budget that covers all aspects of marketing work?
- ☐ Does the school have a strategic marketing plan linked to the school's overall objectives?
- ☐ Is there a comprehensive timetable of marketing activity linked to the school's admission timetable?
- ☐ Are regular progress checks planned?
- ☐ Are there plans to inform and include parents, students and staff in marketing activities?
- ☐ Does the school have the right people internally and the right support from external experts to carry out all the marketing work needed?

CHAPTER THREE: MARKET RESEARCH

Market research can cover a huge area - essentially it involves surveying the rest of the world! However, there are some particularly important areas for marketing - finding out who is most important to the future success of a school, finding out what they want from it and finding out how they like to be communicated with. It should also look at wider changes in the market and see how competitors are responding to the same issues.

a) Stakeholder Analysis

A school is a complex organisation with many people and organisations who can contribute to the overall success of the school. Collectively they are referred to as 'stakeholders'. Some may take up a lot of time and effort, but be relatively unimportant - others may be relatively quiet but important and end up being neglected.

In order to make sure time and effort is focused on the right people, it is possible to divide stakeholders into a number of groups by analysing their **importance** to the future success of the school and their current **interest** in the school. Importance is relatively easy to estimate - which groups have to be involved in the future of the school, and which do not matter? Interest can be measured by looking at whether stakeholders proactively seek to find out about the school or whether they need to be actively contacted.

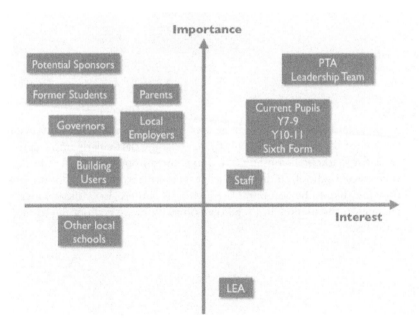

A quick way of developing a picture of stakeholders is to use a matrix like the one above and to invite a representative sample of senior managers and other important members of staff to place Post-It™ notes or similar on the matrix. A possible outcome is shown in the matrix above.

There are three main groups emerging from this analysis. Those who are not important to the future of the school (perhaps an academy school would consider a local authority and other local schools in this area) needs to be kept informed about developments in the simplest possible way - perhaps through news items on the school website or sending them any publications or emailing newsletters.

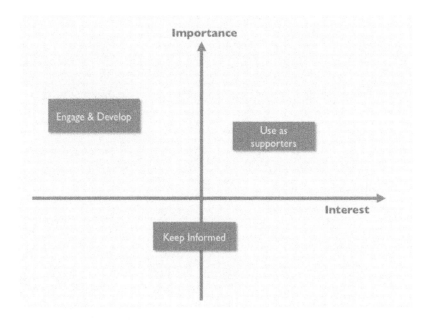

Those who are important and who have a high interest (particularly parents in the PTA, current students and staff, academy chains, and inspection bodies such as OFSTED or the ISI) need to be engaged with and used to help the success of the school as advocates. As we will see below in chapter 6, these groups can provide exciting evidence of success.

Those who are important but have low interest (often the most important and including prospective parents, local faith communities, feeder schools, local employers, estate agents and alumni) need to be actively targeted. The school needs to obtain their contact details and provide regular updates and opportunities to find out more about the school. More details as to how to do this are included in chapters 7 and 8.

b) What do stakeholders want from your school?

Once you have found out the important stakeholders, you need to find out what they want from your school. In the case of supporters, such as parents or current students, there may already be some ways of listening to their needs (such as Parent Voice surveys or a student council). Other stakeholders will be more difficult to research but should not be neglected.

There are two main ways of gathering this information – quantitative **surveys** and qualitative **focus groups.**

Surveys:

Surveys provide an ongoing, quantitative, way of checking stakeholder opinion. They can show how a group of stakeholders feels at a point in time and also allow this to be tracked over time. This can show the impact of marketing and allow you to refine the marketing activity undertaken.

Typical survey questions will include asking how aware the respondent is of a school, what they think the strengths and weaknesses of the school are, what influences or influenced their choice of school to work with, and which media they use to find out about schools. You should also ask for opinions on other schools in the same area or market. A further option would be to ask about wider educational issues or changes you are considering making at your school. As well as being useful when you are looking to make changes to your offering in chapter 4, some of these results may make interesting research that can be used in media relations and publications later.

Surveys can be carried out using different media. Staff can hand out feedback forms at the end of visits, schools can write to, email or telephone selected individuals or ask visitors websites to give their views using free or low cost tools such as SurveyMonkey[3]. For groups you are not in contact with, you can buy mailing lists or arrange for companies to carry out telephone or online surveys.

In all cases it is important to focus on finding out the truth – this is not an exercise in gathering positive comments. The best way is to make the survey anonymous, allow respondents to give a full range of opinions and also allow them to give free comments.

Schools need to remember that by handing out a lot of paper copies someone has to extract and tabulate all the information that is offered by the respondents and then conduct any relevant analysis. Don't underestimate how long this can take! It is important to focus efforts on deciding which questions to ask and then considering and reflecting on the output rather than processing large quantities of data – although remember that in many schools you can draw on the expertise of maths teachers to perform statistical analysis!

Focus groups:

Another good way to gather information is through focus groups of key stakeholders. These are a key qualitative research tool and are useful for investigating softer issues, uncovering in detail the various attitudes and motivations which may exist about a particular issue rather than knowing how many others feel the same.

Focus groups of people who are not supporters of the school will need incentives to take part. This could take the form of direct payment or charitable donations.

The best group for a new marketing leader to start with would be the head teacher and other members of the senior management team. They will be able to clarify what they feel the strengths of the school are as

---

[3] www.surveymonkey.com

well as their vision for the future of the school and changes that are in progress. Talking to other groups such as teachers, parents and students then allows the marketer to see how these strengths are shared. It is best to run a number of groups with participants who have common ground between them (e.g. new parents) rather than creating a large, mixed group.

There are a number of different ways of running these groups, from informal chats over coffee to videoed sessions with expert observers. Expert consultants are often hired to assist with this and using them can also improve the level of validity and robustness, both in positive and negative feedback. An expert facilitator will also be able to ensure that all participants are able to give feedback rather than for example letting one person dominate.

A focus group should be well planned and be based on a discussion guide - a series of open questions which will shape the flow of conversation during the discussion. The moderator needs to keep the group on track (allowing specific issues to be explored where relevant), while probing for as much detail as the respondents are prepared to give. It is difficult to both moderate and record the results of a focus group – try to record the conversation (allowing time to transcribe it later) or have a note taker present to take down general notes and specific quotes and soundbites.

Don't lead participants or make assumptions about what they want from a school – for example from reading some national media it is easy to assume that all parents want traditional, academic schools. You should also accept any issues that stakeholders have with the school in a non-defensive manner. However, try to keep issues general (lack of communication, poor exam results) rather than focusing on the specific issues that for example a parent may have with one teacher (although this should be noted and addressed following the focus group).

At the end of the focus group remember to add general questions about the media the group reads and other ways they find out about schools.

c) Further analysis – segmentation and targeting

One of the most important principles of marketing is that each group of stakeholders can be further divided, put into different groups and targeted with different messages. But what does this mean for a school?

Take the parents of your future intake for example. There are two times to further segment parents - when planning your initial campaign and once information has been gathered from potential parents and students:

1. When planning your campaign.

a) Current parents - In a mixed school, around 50% of applications should be from siblings (assuming 2 children per family. This falls to 25% for single sex schools and goes someway to explaining the trend for private schools going mixed!)

b) Parents who live locally and could choose your school on the basis that it is the easiest one to travel to.

c) Parents in your school's local faith community or at designated 'feeder schools' (if applicable).

d) Parents within a sensible travelling distance who would be interested in specific features of the school (e.g. academic standards, sporting facilities).

e) International parents (for independent/boarding schools) or those relocating to the local area.

Each of these groups can be approached in different ways and will also need a different combination of messages. For example current parents with siblings are easy to identify and you can write to them directly or arrange personal meetings. Those relocating to the area might involve working with local estate agents or large employers. Different prospectus inserts or specific web 'landing' pages could also be created for each group.

Within the content also make sure that the case studies used reflect the target audience and that key benefits for each group are emphasised - local parents will be far more interested in transport issues while those applying from abroad to a boarding school may want to know about support for English language development!

If you have time and money at this stage there are a number of powerful analysis tools that help you find areas that contain potential parents by postcode or street – such as MTM Consulting's MANDARIN product[4].

2. During the campaign.

Once the first Open Day has been held or a number of parents have visited the school it is possible to segment them further based on what they want most from the school, especially if you ask them to fill in a survey when visiting. Possible segments might then include:

a) Academic focus
b) Sporting focus
c) Musical focus
d) Pastoral/SEN focus

For private schools, it is worth splitting those who would be dependent on financial support from the school into another segment as well.

Make sure sporty parents are sent details of sporting events, news of success in tournaments and so on, while musical parents are invited to concerts! There's nothing new about this process of course, as the presence of sporting and musical bursaries in private schools shows!

---

[4] http://www.mtmconsulting.co.uk/research/#Mandarin

As always with marketing, make sure to reflect back regularly on decisions and check that prospective parents are responding to the segments chosen.

d) How can you communicate best with stakeholders?

Both surveys and focus groups will identify the types of media (and individual newspaper and magazine titles and websites) that influence stakeholders. Try to be as specific as possible when asking.

Once a list of the most important media has been produced it is important to subscribe to them and read them regularly. This will help external market research (see below), inform conversations with advertisers and enable you to find key journalists to talk to if you start a media relations programme.

As well as print and online media, make sure you know of other ways that stakeholders communicate – for example parents will discuss your school at the 'school gate' of feeder schools, in playgroups, their faith communities, family gatherings and at sporting events. You can't listen in directly to these you should use market research (formal and informal) to find out what is being said about your school – the best way of overcoming any negative impressions is to make sure that you are producing positive stories about your school and making as many people as possible aware of them.

e) External Market Research

It is important to be in touch with other developments that will affect your school and allow it to differentiate itself from other schools. There are a number of different things you need to be monitoring.

One well-known external market research analytical tool is a PEST analysis. PEST stands for Political, Economic, Social and Technological (some business writers add in Legal and Environmental). The aim is to focus on the key areas where change is happening that can affect your organisation.

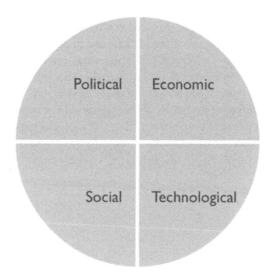

- Political changes in education are regular and on a large scale. In recent years, changes in school status, the role of Local Authorities, inspection routines, league tables, new exams and changing attitudes to staff pay and unions are all major issues that affect schools.

- Economic changes are also highly important – for example many areas are still feeling the effect of the recent recession while others have recovered quickly and parents may be more able to afford private education.

- Social changes include demographic shifts, such as the ongoing baby boom, as well as immigration and changing attitudes to learning among students and their parents.

- Technological change also is impacting strongly on education, moving well beyond the equipment used to teach to include new ways of teaching and learning – and new distractions for students!

How is this done?

The best way is to find the media, organisations and networks that cover your particular type of school and subscribe to their magazines, publications and social media networks. This should include media such as:

- TES (Times Educational Supplement)[5]
- SecEd magazine (for those in secondary education)[6]
- Education Guardian (published Tuesdays)[7]

---

[5] tes.co.uk

[6] sec-ed.co.uk

[7] guardian.co.uk

- The Independent Schools Magazine (for private schools)[8]
- Prep School magazine[9]
- Local newspapers and magazines aimed at parents

You should also subscribe to publications and emails from networking groups, join social media groups and attend conferences and other meetings.

Organisations to network through include:

School leader networks:

- The Schools Network (who produce the highly useful SSAT Policy Radar)
- Headmasters Conference (for private schools)
- ISC (Independent Schools Council), which produces a highly useful annual Census based on feedback from private schools.

School marketing networks:

- AMDIS (UK marketing network for private schools)
- InspiredSM.com (US school marketing network for all schools)
- Marketing Advice for Schools (UK based network)

---

[8] independentschoolsmagazine.co.uk

[9] prepschoolmag.co.uk

Useful and active Twitter feeds include:

- @SchoolDuggery (probably the best connected education tweeter!)
- @goodSchools (the Good Schools Guide)
- @schoolsimprove (a useful link to education stories in the media)

If you have access to local or national politicians (such as a councillor on your Governing Body or a well-connected parent), make sure that you talk to them about changes that are coming.

You need to develop a system of filing key information. This could take the form of a cuttings file, or you could use technology such as Evernote[10] to allow you to index and access news from different electronic platforms.

You can track most of the relevant media coverage online or by subscribing to local media yourself, but you can also employ media tracking organisations such as Gorkana[11] to scan publications for you and find key words.

---

[10] evernote.com

[11] gorkana.com

f) Competitor Research

Schools, private and state, have historically been reluctant to think of each other as competitors. It's true that we all share a common goal to educate children and that perhaps, in another political environment or country, competition would not exist.

But today's school leaders don't have the luxury to take this moral high ground. All schools, whether state or independent are competing against each other. Private schools that fail to attract enough income will close (unless perhaps they convert to free schools); state schools that don't out-perform their peers will be shown up in league tables and forced to convert to academies (or increasingly change academy chain); new free schools cannot expect to be supported if they are not recruiting new pupils. In this environment it's hardly a surprise that the UK House of Commons Education Select Committee found that schools aren't helping each other[12].

The first step to thriving in a competitive environment is to work out how you are different from other schools. This allows you to market yourself on your strengths - and to identify the areas that are seen as weaknesses. How do you do this? Here's a quick and easy process to get you started:

1. Work out who your competitors are.

List up to 10 schools that you know parents consider as alternatives. If you're not sure, make sure you ask your current parents on a regular basis. Remember that there are probably different competitors if you have different stages of your school, from private nurseries to Sixth Form and FE Colleges.

---

[12] bbc.co.uk/news/education-24821378

2. Set up your research.

Create a table and against each school create three headings –
'Strengths', 'Reasons to choose [my school]' and 'Marketing
Thoughts'.

3. Analyse strengths.

Look at the websites and other marketing material that other schools
produce and write down what they are projecting as their strengths -
examples would be academic progress, facilities, pastoral support or
wider student development. Make a note of fees charged if the school
is private.

4. Create your response.

In the next column write down the key (positive) messages you would
use to persuade prospective parents not to go to that school. Examples
would be 'we're nearer / cheaper / more pastorally focused'.

5. Learn from competitors.

In the final column write down anything that has impressed you about
how these schools market themselves - imitation is the sincerest form
of flattery! They might use excellent photography or convey a very
clear and consistent message through different media.

Once you've analysed your stakeholders, the external market and your
competition you're in the best position to work out what you need to
do to compete – in the next chapter.

Chapter checklist...

☐ Have you analysed your stakeholders and found who is most important?

☐ Do you talk regularly to parents and other key stakeholders and gather information from them?

☐ Do you know what media key stakeholders read and trust and what other sources of information they use?

☐ Are you an active member of local and national education networks?

☐ Do you read and capture information from local, specialist and national media to inform your marketing?

☐ Are you aware of the strengths, weaknesses and messages used by your competition?

CHAPTER FOUR: MEETING MARKET NEEDS

Marketing is not about just taking an existing product and selling it – the product or service itself must meet the needs of the customer. This is where this section of the book is important – once you have gathered information about your customers and competition, you need to assess your offering and see what needs to be changed to create competitive difference and advantage.

This section of the **Marketing Cycle** is closely related to the strategic development of the school and provides another key reason for marketing being represented on the Senior Leadership Team of a school. The 'market position' of the school is an important strategic planning tool and many of the 'marketing' issues that can be changed in response are related to the curriculum, teaching and learning or financial management.

a) How does your offer meet the needs of the market?

Following your market research above you will have a lot of information about the school, and about the needs of your stakeholders. You can analyse this using a SWOT framework – strengths, weaknesses, opportunities and threats.

Strengths and weaknesses are internal to the school and will come from your survey and focus group research. They usually cover areas such as academic and pastoral issues, community relationships and facilities. It is important to be honest at this stage about weaknesses that are found in market research – it may be that the school has made strides to change an aspect of its performance but perceptions are vital when dealing with external audiences and changes may not have been effectively communicated.

Opportunities and threats are external – they are driven by the findings of your PEST and competitor analyses.

Excerpt from a sample SWOT analysis

Strengths	Weaknesses
Strong local connections	Poor recent academic results
New Sixth Form building	Undersubscribed last year
Opportunities	**Threats**
Partnership with FE college	Free school opening nearby
Local population rising	Nearest school has better results

You should compare your completed SWOT to the desires and needs of parents and other stakeholders. Is there anything you are not offering that many want? Do you offer things that parents are unaware of? You may also find that you are focusing your communications on areas that they are not interested in!

b) What can you change about what you offer?

When marketing professionals started thinking about changing their offerings to meet market needs, they came up with the idea of the 'marketing mix' or '4Ps' – changing product, price, place and promotion. There are a number of different variants to this model, but one that works well for service organisations such as schools where the 'product' is difficult to see is the '7P' framework. This covers the following aspects:

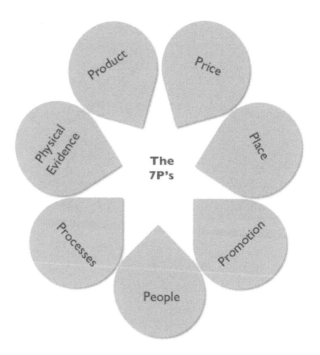

- **Product** – This covers all the operational aspects of a school – teaching, learning, pastoral support and so on. Making changes to how a school works will be out of the hands of marketing professionals but need to be fed back to operational managers for consideration. Examples might include parents wanting new subjects or extra-curricular activities or greater access to their children's progress reports. Market research can also help senior operational managers prioritise changes they are considering making – which ones are most desired?

- **Price** – not so much an issue for state schools, but there may be concerns over uniform, transport or other costs – or for Sixth Forms the alternative attraction of earning a wage. Private schools need to be competitive in their market and also have the opportunity to offer bursaries and scholarships to attract talented individuals.

- **Place** – schools tend to be in a fixed place, but can you offer extra support by improving transport links, using new technology or opening at different times (e.g. by providing wrap-around care or a summer school)?

- **Promotion** – Are stakeholders fully aware of how your school is changing? Are you communicating the right messages? By entering into a marketing programme you will have started changing this aspect.

- **Physical evidence** – the success of a school is most clearly shown in the students who attend the school and have recently graduated. Prospective parents and other stakeholders need to be given the opportunity to learn about these students whether through case studies (see chapter 6) or by meeting them and asking them questions. Physical evidence also covers the way the school looks to visitors and how people are treated when they communicate with the school.

- **People** – are the people that stakeholders meet well trained in how to communicate with them?

- **Processes** – do stakeholders know how to work with the school? For example, is the admissions process easy to understand? Can parents easily make contact with a class teacher or report absence?

Some of these changes are around communication of the current 'product', in particular promotion and physical evidence. Some are major changes that require insight from operational managers and senior leaders. However, this model does show that marketing is integral to all changes that take place in a school and underlines the importance of having a marketing representative at the top of a school's organisational structure.

It is difficult to give specific examples of all the changes that can be made in a school – but here are two examples of how innovation in service provision and communication can make a difference to a school.

c) Examples of change

A. Improving Sixth Form Recruitment

In the past the expectation was that students stayed at the same school where possible from 11 to 18. However, Sixth Form and Further Education Colleges that have to recruit half their students every year have developed good marketing programmes. Students are coming up to their GCSE results in August aware that they have options and keen to exercise their right to choose.

In many areas, the colleges are winning the battle – because they are the ones listening to students and giving them what they are asking for. They are using their economies of scale to offer the facilities students want – from well-equipped video and recording studios to high class sporting teams. They are attracting the best teachers from 11-18 schools ('No Y9! Great!') and let their large department teams focus on teaching 2 year groups rather than 7. They emphasis the social benefits of having just 2 year groups present. They have relaxed rules on uniform and a university-like focus on learning over appearance (the one I worked in was a sea of red hair and piercings…).

Oh, and they are targeting parents. Schools don't realise this and think that students are making the choice in isolation, but the colleges have spent a lot of time and energy trying to remove any fears that parents have of a poorer education. They push their high positions in league tables (check out Farnborough, Hills Road, Cambridge and Winstanley Colleges for example), they emphasise their pastoral and discipline support ('we don't let them slack off') and they offer careers advice to match the best school Sixth Forms. They also directly target parental concerns – for example by inviting parents in for 'parental information days' where they address many of the issues discussed above.

What can a schools do in response? Here are a few suggestions:

1. Listen to your Y10 and Y11 students.

Don't assume that they are happy with the transition to your Sixth Form. Carry out focus groups and interviews early and encourage honesty. Ask them to suggest a 'top ten' of what they'd like to see in your Sixth Form and take the opportunity to find out how they are researching alternatives – what media are going to influence their choices? You can use the same media to recruit students from other schools.

2. Listen to parents.

Set up some focus groups to find out what parents *really* think of your Sixth Form and other alternatives. What are their concerns? Talk to some parents who sent students to other schools – why did they do this?

3. Research the competition.

How are colleges and other Sixth Forms selling their services? Do you have copies of their prospectuses? Do you know what they say at interviews (ask some of your students if not)? How do they make themselves distinctive?

4. Innovate.

What can you offer to parents and students that will differentiate your school? Examples include offering curriculum innovations such as the International Baccalaureate or Pre-U or supplementary studies such as the Extended Project Qualification or the Open University's YASS courses. **And don't be afraid to think the unthinkable.** You are allowed to add vocational subjects and relax your dress code!

5. Sell the benefits of your Sixth Form by using Sixth Formers.

Link your Y10 and Y11 students to Sixth Formers and let them see what it's really like to be in a Sixth Form. This can take the form of lesson shadowing, teambuilding events, joint sporting events or even something as simple as holding joint assemblies. Do the same with parents and external candidates – let your Sixth Formers take the lead in any Y10 and Y11 events (including Parents Evenings!) and develop case studies of your best Sixth Formers for use in wider media. Have you thought of setting up a blog where a few selected Sixth Formers can talk of their experiences?

6. Keep communicating.

Make sure all potential students and parents know your Sixth Form results, the innovations you are making and the facilities on offer – and don't forget your current students. Make sure you communicate these benefits repeatedly through your prospectus, advertising website and social media (really important for talking to students!).

7. Make it personal for both current students and external ones!

Arrange to talk to all current parents and students at the start of Y11. Listen to any individual concerns and let them know if you can address them as soon as possible. And once someone displays interest in your school from outside, make sure you get their contact details and keep talking to them.

B. Recruiting the best teachers

In order for a school to succeed it seems clear that it must have the best teachers available. Yet in May 2014 there were over 7,000 jobs advertised on the most popular UK teaching jobs website tes.co.uk and in August 2014 32% of school governors reported 'struggling to recruit classroom teachers'[13].

While there are two important HR-led tasks in staff recruitment - working out the skills needed for the role and identifying the best person for the job from a pool of applicants, there is also two vital marketing roles – creating the right environment (meeting market needs) and attracting the right people to apply (marketing communications).

As in any marketing task you need to consider who you'd like to apply and what would attract them - and then work out the best media to use. You also need to make sure your advert is different and persuasive!

1. Realise that you're selling!

If you need an experienced teacher you'll probably have to persuade someone to move from an existing job, which they may be happy in. If you want an NQT (newly qualified teacher), they will have the choice of many schools perhaps from around the country. You need to stand out.

2. Set out what you offer first, not what you expect.

Make the job sound attractive from the start. Almost all teaching adverts start by asking for teachers who are 'outstanding' (or occasionally 'enthusiastic' or 'innovative'). Apart from being unrealistic

---

[13] 'Schools have the jobs, so where are the staff?', TES, 15th August 2014

(we can't all be outstanding!), if you start by talking about how your school <u>helps</u> teachers to become outstanding you'll get much more interest.

Similarly, adverts often talk at length about why the school is great for students and parents by quoting OFSTED or ISI grades, but forget that they're trying to attract great teachers who may be looking for flexible working, professional development or just a happy department.

3. Be flexible and creative in your use of media.

Don't just put an ad in the TES and sit back. By definition it's only teachers who are actively looking for work that take time to read job websites - there are probably many others who would love to work for your school. Think about other media that are used by teachers, as well as the existing marketing materials you use, your social media and your community links. If you keep lists of people who have applied speculatively in the past, email them about the job. If you don't keep these lists - start one. Make sure you let your staff and parents know what you're looking for as well.

4. Make the application process welcoming.

For someone already in a job, applying for a new one is optional and a chore. Don't let them think of this by wasting space reminding them of the need for 3 references, an application form and covering letter, proof of current address and so on - teachers expect this. It's much better to start the process by inviting people to call for an informal chat or visit. You can also think about reducing the information needed on an application form (do you really need all GCSE grades for example?)

5. Support your advert with evidence that you're a good employer.

Set up a recruitment page on your website with evidence of training and development and genuine interviews with current employees. If you're part of a chain, check whether they are already doing this.

6. Be courteous and realise the effort it takes to apply for a job.

It doesn't take long for word to get out if you're rude or arrogant and a poor reputation as a recruiter can last for a long time. I've been asked by a number of colleagues and former colleagues about whether to apply to particular schools over the years and I know very quickly which ones I would discourage - the school that invited me for an informal chat then never made contact again, the school that asked me to reapply for a job when they got around to readvertising it, 'in case we don't find anyone more suitable' (for which read better), the training organisation that forgot to pay a friend of mine on numerous occasions.

On the other hand, I'd highly recommend two schools that didn't offer me a job - because they treated me well even if they found someone better.

Chapter checklist...

- ☐ Have you summarised your current offering using the **SWOT** framework?
- ☐ Have you identified gaps in communication and in service offering that need to fill?
- ☐ Have you attempted to fill in these gaps, working with operational managers and teachers to create innovation?

CHAPTER FIVE: MESSAGE AND BRAND DEVELOPMENT

Once you know what your school needs to say to the wider market, you need to work out how to show this clearly and communicate it consistently. This chapter takes you through the process of constructing visual imagery and written messages which will lead to focused communications internally and externally.

a) What is a brand?

A brand was originally something stamped on an animal to show ownership! Now it is much more. A good definition is that the brand is the whole customer experience of a product or service. As Howard Schultz, CEO of Starbucks said, "Starbucks represents something beyond a cup of coffee"[14]. You can pay 50p for a coffee in a cafe, so why pay £3.00 in Starbucks for a chemically similar milky brown liquid?

For a school, the brand is the whole experience of what it is like for a child to spend several years in a school, during which time they mature and change enormously.

The challenge set in this chapter is distilling this down into short written and verbal messages and pictures that quickly show how you are different from and better than other schools. Once you have done this, you can start filling in the gaps, adding evidence (chapter 6), letting the wider world know the messages (chapter 7) and answering the specific needs and concerns of those who respond (chapter 8).

---

[14] brainyquote.com/quotes/authors/h/howard_schultz.html

b) Creating written and verbal messages – the 'brand pyramid'

Imagine that you are in a lift with a prospective parent. They mention that they have a 9 year old child and haven't decided which secondary school to send them to (if you work in a primary school, they've got a 2-year-old!). You have 30 seconds until they reach their floor to start the process of making them choose your school. What do you say to gain their interest in your school? Would every member of your staff be able to make the same key points? Would it be consistent with your advertising material and website?

You need to use the information you've gathered in the chapters above from the school's vision, strengths and innovations, stakeholder, market and competitor research and add the experience of staff and students at the school and the school's vision for the future to distil the key strengths of the school in four different ways as laid out in the 'brand pyramid' triangle below. This is something that takes time, but is incredibly worthwhile. It is the combination of strengths, innovations and vision that counts.

The first stage is to put together a team from around the school to do this – an external facilitator might help, but schools can also do this for themselves. An idea team should involve senior managers, governors, parents and students.

Starting at the bottom of the pyramid you need to identify 10 to 20 bullet points that cover the things that your school is good at. At this stage, you must ignore negative thoughts! It may be that the school has been through a difficult time and that the current 'brand' is not strong. The key here is to focus on the most positive things already happening at the school alongside your aspirations. For example, the school may have had poor exam results but it might also be a very friendly, responsive community school with strong aspirations and new approaches to learning – attractive to many parents!

Then look at which of these (in combination) make you unique. Which ones can be backed up by strong evidence or are your most important aspirations? You might settle on three, four or perhaps five bullet points. Read these back to the group and see if most people agree on them – and that no other school could claim to do the same. Don't worry about trying again if one or more of them is rejected. These are your 'Unique Selling Points' (USPs) and need to be repeatedly referred to across all your communications.

Once you know the key points, use different words and phrases to get them across in a couple of sentences – the 'elevator pitch' mentioned at the start of the section. While you are looking to keep the overall messages short, there is no specific number of words to stick to!

Finally, think about a short 'slogan' that takes the most important part of the 'elevator pitch' into a few words.

If might take a couple of hours to reach an initial consensus – you might then want to reflect on this over a period of a few days, involving the wider school community. Having gone through this process with a number of organisations myself, the more people you can involve the better the result seems to be - and this is reflected in the greater support from people in the organisation to the success of the marketing activity.

You can look at schools you admire in your local area to identify similar key messages. Here are a few examples to inspire you:

Manchester Grammar School:

What makes your school unique?

'Where able boys from all backgrounds come together to pursue their passion for learning. Where boys find unparalleled excellence in and beyond the classroom. And where, since 1515, boys of today have become men of the future'[15].

Slogan: 'Join the Adventure'

Wellington School, Altrincham

What makes your school unique?

'High standards are expected of all our students and staff. All of our work is anchored in the values of mutual respect, responsibility, discipline, care for the individual and high achievement.'[16]

Slogan: 'Excellence in Everything'

Also consider drafting some guidelines on writing. These should include guide to the way the school describes itself, the language used in schools (a common issue is whether the school has 'students', 'learners' or 'pupils' for example) and also an idea of the type of tone

---

[15]mgs.org/ (quoted 8/6/2012)

[16] wellington.trafford.sch.uk/ (quoted 8/6/2012)

and voice that should be used. This is very useful when a large number of individuals write for the school website or publications.

The next challenge is to provide the evidence to back up your claims. Chapter 6 explains how to get these examples.

c) How St Bede's College used 'Wordles' to find key messages

CASE STUDY from marketingadviceforschools.com

A visual depiction of the words in a text'. That's the formal definition of a 'wordle'. For me it's a lot more than that. It's a way of quickly getting to the heart of the strengths of an organisation, the needs of customers, or the preoccupations of a writer.

Take the 'wordle' above. This is the result of a short minute exercise with a group of Sixth Form students at St Bede's College in Manchester. They were simply asked to write down three words that described the advantages of studying science at that particular school. Putting the words directly into wordle.net (and a bit of enjoyable playing with fonts and colours) generated the picture above.

What stands out? 'Supportive', 'challenging' and 'fun' spring out -

followed by 'good relationships' and perhaps unexpectedly 'explosions (but then they all studied Chemistry A-level)'. From here you're already half way to the key messages. Our first 'key message' was 'the school gives a lot of support to students while challenging them to succeed - and it does this in an exciting environment'.

The process that started with this wordle was extended to cover a wide range of stakeholders in the school and resulted in the key message statement below...

> "*Our mission*
> is to inspire, encourage
> and enable every one
> of our pupils to change
> the world by fulfilling
> their role in it."

...with the slogan 'inspiring pupils from 3-18'.

Once we'd come up with an idea of the message our task was to find the evidence to back it up - case studies of current students details of the support given (such as small class size, revision sessions or online support), profiles of the teachers who provide the academic and pastoral support - and of course photos and videos of those explosions!

Finally, one other advantage was that we were able to directly feedback the findings to the students – to show them how they directly contributed to the research and how much their opinions matter to the school!

d) Creating a visual identity

EXPERT ADVICE from marketingadviceforschools.com

By Helen West, designer and Director at Wests Design (wests-design.com)

As with message development, this is an area where you should consider investing in external design consultants or using your own expert in the art or graphics department.

The starting point is the brand identity or logo. In some cases schools may have a long-established crest or coat of arms which may benefit from a minor refresh. For other schools, such as newly opened academies, an entirely new identity may be required. The identity needs to reflect what the school stands for.

In thinking about the school logo or identity, some key tips for success include:

- Define a primary palette of colours - around 4 would be ideal - which you stick to. Each of these colours will have a number of specific references (ie. Pantone, CMYK and RGB for printing, RAL for paint and HEX for digital applications) which will ensure they always appear consistently.
- Consider existing historical representations of the school - what do they say to people e.g. mottos, badges - are they relevant?
- Keep it simple – consider how easily the logo can be reproduced onto signage or uniform and how much impact it will have when seen alongside the branding of other schools. The detail in overly detailed designs will be lost, whilst basic designs run the risk of looking crude or juvenile.

Once the logo has been agreed (either refreshing an existing one or creating a new one from scratch), the next challenge is to apply it to a range of collateral – after all, the logo is rarely seen in isolation, but needs to work as well on uniform as it does on letterheads and in press adverts. These 'design elements' are summarised in the next section of the book.

Developing a series of designs for all the elements which need to be brought 'on brand' is a task most effectively delegated to a specialist designer. Having professional input at this stage ensures that the whole suite of marketing materials retains a consistent and professional appearance. It also enables the styling to be sense-checked objectively for usability (e.g. not using colours which clash, making sure that all text is legible and incorporating consistent fonts).

Some schools work with a freelance graphic designer to keep costs down, rather than contracting a marketing consultancy. A pragmatic approach is to commission the designer to create templates for a number of areas and to then develop these internally if you have skills and resources available.

The list below is not exhaustive as but is a good starting point of collateral for a school intending to rebrand.

The final stage, once all these elements have been created, is to compile them into a set of basic brand guidelines. This document summarises the templates and specifics of all core elements of the visual branding, from the logo, fonts and colour palette, to advertising concepts. It doesn't need to be too complex or lengthy (around 8-10 pages maximum) but will help ensure consistency of brand delivery.

One final suggestion is that you build up a library of photographs that cover the likely needs of marketing communications activities. This is likely to initially include pictures of buildings and senior staff members, and to be added to as new stories, experts and case studies are developed. However, the reality is that pictures of happy and engaged pupils will be more successful at selling any school than photos of facilities or teachers. With this in mind some useful points to consider include:

- natural / 'in situ' ' 'reportage' shots work are often more powerful than staged 'smiling to camera' photos
- all images must have the necessary permissions and adhere to safeguarding best practice
- remember that pupils develop and their appearance can change significantly over 1 or 2 years so expect to replace photos on a regular basis (there's nothing worse than using images in marketing of children who have already left the school!).

e) Design elements for a school

Element	Notes
Signage	It is relatively costly to replace signage on-site but look tactically at changing the more prominent signs as it can have huge impact
Website	Designing a new look and feel for your website homepage and other key pages demonstrates how the branding will be brought to life digitally. If budgets are tight and you have skills available, you could consider having the homepage designed professionally and then delegate the application of this template to someone within your team
Prospectus	Some schools outsource the design of the entire prospectus, whilst others may get the cover and 'style setters' for the opening pages designed professionally and then replicate this look and feel themselves as they populate it with content
Laminated Card Folder	Many schools use branded folders made from laminated card to package together loose materials for distribution to parents (eg. progress reports, new starter information, etc.) They typically have a folded or glued flap on the inner section to carry paperwork. Folders can carry branded design and impactful photography across 4 sides and are a cost effective yet very corporate way of getting the branded message out to target audiences.
School stationery	You need to think about letterheads, compliments slips, business cards, ID cards, branded lanyards, etc. Make sure you consider which accreditations or awards you

Element	Notes
	want to feature as some may date or become obsolete. Letterheads can be set up as Word documents and then printed off when required, as well as having a stock of pre-printed paper.
Document templates	You need to set up branded templates for all documents generated within school, including memos, briefing notes, Powerpoint masters, invoices, report covers, etc. Don't forget email sign-offs – once the content has been agreed they can be set up by the IT team to appear automatically.
Advertising templates	Applying the branding to external marketing materials is ideally a job for a professional designer. You need to think about clarity of layout, hierarchy of message (ie. what are the main things you want your target audience to take out of the advert), the call to action (what response to the advert are you seeking). You also need to think about the styling of headlines, the use of imagery, etc. You aren't looking for finished adverts, but concepts which can be developed when required using the right photos and messaging.
Interior environments	Branding isn't just on a page or a school badge – the schools which really embrace their brand translate it from 2D into 3D and bring it to life through their school environment. Examples include wall and window décor, reception areas, etc
Uniform	Don't underestimate the time and effort it takes to change your uniform! To manage the process smoothly, pupils, parents, staff and governors all need to be consulted. There needs to be a reasonable lead time to give people sufficient notice, especially

Element	Notes
	parents who have to finance the items and want to get maximum longevity from their investment. However, the introduction of a different coloured sweatshirt to tie in with your new branding may be achievable within a school year and can bring the brand to life more effectively than anything.

f) How St Mary's created a new visual identity

CASE STUDY from marketingadviceforschools.com

St Mary's R.C. Primary School, Levenshulme is a mid-sized state primary in a suburb of Manchester. The catchment is fairly mixed, with a higher than average proportion of pupils receiving free school meals (FSM) and having English as an additional language (EAL). A new Headteacher was appointed in 2011, bringing a renewed vision and a fresh perspective to this well-established voluntary-aided school.

One of the first things to be commissioned from a local designer was a new logo, designed to symbolise the Christian beliefs which underpin the ethos of the school and the exciting new vision being unveiled. The previous identity was a traditional design, paired with a staid burgundy and yellow colour palette. In comparison the new design depicts an angel with open wings in a bold and more contemporary palette.

Previous logo

New logo

The fresh colour theme was applied to all communication materials, from a basic Word template which could be applied to all policies, to new letterhead and compliments slips and branded stickers for exercise books.

A new website was designed and launched which has proved very popular with all members of the school community. It is kept up to date and conveys the bright, open feel of the school.

When budget permitted, external signage was replaced with huge impact, together with the use of coloured vinyls onto windows to bring the branding to life for the pupils and staff throughout the site. Finally, a new uniform was launched (navy sweatshirts to replace the previous burgundy ones).

In summary, significant changes in teaching and learning were already well underway at St Mary's, but investing in these visual changes has accelerated the transformation of the school by actively demonstrating, internally and externally, a new vision and aspirations. Pupils, parents, staff and governors can readily articulate the considerable changes that have taken place, which has maintained momentum and built engagement.

New signage

New door imagery

f) Aligning parents, staff and students behind the new messages and design

Before you use the new messages and identify, you must let parents, staff and students have a chance to get to know the key messages and to give their feedback. All three groups are excellent salespeople for your school, but if they contradict key messages because they don't know about them, other stakeholders will wonder how deeply they run. Constant feedback at all stages of the process will help with this, as will openness to their thoughts – don't be too rigid with working on images until the very end.

One way to achieve this is to set up a 'marketing table' in staff rooms which you can also put out for parents on parent consultation evenings and other events. You can display ideas, marketing materials, design concepts and articles – and leave lots of Post-It notes for comments, ideas and so on. Make sure to thank those giving you ideas as well!

You should also consider the way your school looks to visitors. It might not be possible to replace all signage or repaint the school in your new colours immediately, but you should aim to do this as soon as possible.

It is of course vital that the 'brand message' is 'lived' by all members of staff, especially senior managers.

Chapter checklist...

- ☐ Have you identified the key messages that you want to communicate and a short 'slogan' to use in all advertising?
- ☐ Have you created a 5-minute 'elevator pitch' that contains these messages?
- ☐ Do you have a clear and consistent set of guidelines for visual communication?
- ☐ Do you have photographs of key people, buildings and other important images?
- ☐ Have you presented new messages and design to students, staff and parents and let them give constructive feedback?

CHAPTER SIX: GATHERING EVIDENCE

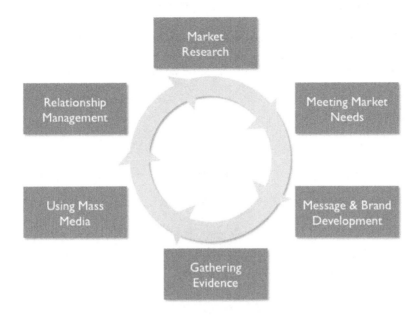

I recently asked the Head of a leading independent school how long it would take him to find five students who exemplified the key values that his marketing material was claiming. 'Five minutes', he replied. 'Then why aren't they in your marketing material?' I replied.

The reason for my rudeness was that once you have decided the key messages that you want to communicate, you need to gather evidence that these messages are real or at the very least a serious aspiration and **the only long term way of doing this in a trust-based environment such as a school is to provide hard evidence that you deliver what you say is special about your school.**

While there may be many examples of more ephemeral products that have been marketed in a 'clever' way, few people will choose a school for their children based on gimmicks or slogans.

There are many types of evidence that can be communicated, but they can be divided into four major areas. Once evidence is gathered, it can be used in many different ways as outlined in Chapters 7 and 8.

a) News stories

Schools are full of new stories. Any community of hundreds of people will include fascinating items of news on a daily basis. You need to be able to find these stories, identify the ones that support your key messages and or of most interest to your stakeholders and gather information in a timely fashion. Depending on the size of your school and your resources you should aim to always use between one and five stories a week.

How can you do this? You need to think like a good journalist on a local newspaper. You need to encourage people throughout the school community to let you know what they are doing, and you need to proactively spend time in all parts of the community.

A lot of the information you gather will be about future events ranging from formal results days (see later in this chapter) to class trips, charity events or visiting speakers. You should create a formal events calendar from this and use it to produce around half the news stories you need. The rest of the stories will be immediate – perhaps a student has won a national award or produced some great project work.

If you're stuck for ideas as to what good news looks like, try following the Good News from Schools (@goodnews_schls) Twitter feed, which is now part of marketingadviceforschools.com. It aims to share the best things that schools do – in part so that other schools can see the value in capturing news stories.

If on the other hand, you find you have lots of stories and not enough time to capture them it is fine to focus on the most 'newsworthy'. Stories about external prizes or student achievements are always going to be more interesting than internal awards for example.

Setting up a Student News Team

A great way of increasing your marketing resources and linking marketing to the wider student body is to create a student news team. In some schools, journalistic activities can be used to support the curriculum, while in others students will develop useful additional skills.

To set up a student news team you should work with teachers (especially in the English and Art/Photography departments in a secondary school) to identify students who would be suitable for this exercise.

Arrange to meet the students at the same time and the same place each week. In the first meeting it is helpful to discuss the role of a journalist and outline the stories that you would like them to gather. You can assign different roles to different students (photographer, journalist, sub-editor), although they should all be looking for stories that they can bring along to the meetings.

At subsequent meetings you can bring along a list of story ideas that you have, but you should also listen to ideas from the students. Set a sensible target number of stories to follow up, and make sure that you check with other members of staff before sending along a student reporter to an activity.

When you discuss stories, which ones do you pick? As stated above the key factors are consistency with your key messages and interest to stakeholders. You should try to produce at least one story per month to support each key message that you have decided on. Within this framework, again thinking like a journalist, you are looking for a 'hook' – something that is different and exciting about the story. This story might be unique, it might be on a large scale, it might be highly unusual, or it might involve someone who has overcome personal challenges.

Examples of news stories include new buildings, exam results, sporting fixtures, drama productions, academic achievements, club projects, awards evenings, musical evenings, guest lectures, charity fundraising, school trips, students or teachers appearing as experts in the media, and much more.

However, you should make sure news items are related to the school. Publicising the out-of-school achievements of a student or teacher can be a waste of time, unless they can attribute some of that success to the school.

A final point - it is also important to tell stories internally via the school newsletter or website so that those in the story are aware that they have been featured.

b) Making the most of Results Day – an example of a news story

There are two times each year when secondary schools can guarantee everyone is interested in them – A-level and GCSE Results Days in mid-August.

While the national media focus on the raw numbers and try to explain how better and worse results mean students aren't as clever as they used to, local papers, current and prospective parents and others in the local community are more interested in personal stories of success that show how your school has helped individuals.

However, people aren't going to see these stories without a bit of help! Follow the steps below to get your messages out there.

1. Prepare

You should work with your school's Pastoral team (Heads of Year, Head of Sixth Form etc.) to identify the most newsworthy stories. These aren't only the students likely to achieve the highest grades – newspapers are also interested in students who have overcome significant personal challenges or have made a lot of progress in a short time. You should write short case studies well in advance (include details of the students' background, current subjects, likely university/college place/job/predicted grades) and ask their parents (or the students themselves if over 18) for permission to use them in marketing activity.

2. Encourage students to come to school on Results Day

With the trend toward texting results and making them available online, students may not come into school and may just drift to college or university. You can make results day more special by offering refreshments to students and parents at a specific time, and by encouraging (popular) teaching staff to attend. You can also attract students by ensuring that you have sufficient teachers and other staff to advise on UCAS/careers decisions. You should invite your 'case study' students personally.

3. Research your media in advance

Check how all the media that are important to you are covering Results Day. Alex Scatens from the *Sale & Altrincham Advertiser* suggests calling local papers' news desks a couple of weeks in advance of results day to check the paper's plans for coverage and let them know your arrangements. You can also let the paper know of your interesting stories. The national press are starting to formalise the process of finding stories – the *Guardian* for example asks schools to submit results online along with possible case studies.

4. The day before

The School Exams Officer and senior school management have access to results the day before they are released. Actual results cannot be shared with anyone outside of this group but they can pick out the highlights that reflect your school's priorities, and write a general news release, as well as inserting the stories that you have prepared. Leave space for comments from students.

If a student you have written a case study of has failed to meet their expectations or UCAS offer, it is best to leave it out of your initial media release – but you can talk to them and make changes on the day. Just in case it needed saying – you are NOT allowed to communicate results to students or the media before 6am on the actual results date.

5. Get in early on Results Day

Exam boards will not issue any overall results to the media until 9.30 am on results day although results can be released to students from 6am – it's not essential to be up then though! You can then fill in online surveys and email stories to your selected media (even if they've promised to turn up, it's a lot easier to adapt an email that rewrite a paper copy). Once students start to turn up, you can talk to them and add their comments and reactions to your copy (please be sensitive though – even if they've achieved their expected grades, they are going to be emotional!)

6. Take photos and video

Alex Scatens points out that a local paper will not be able to send a photographer to every school, but that they will consider using good quality pictures that you email in. They are also vital for you to use elsewhere. Video interviews of students are also very useful and can be quickly edited and posted on YouTube, your website and other places. Try to take photos of genuine celebrations – and again make sure you have permission from those in the picture to use them! If you have a group of students who have done well (e.g. your 'Oxbridge' students), prioritise taking a photo with them all together.

7. Remember to use all media channels

You should put the stories and pictures on your website, your social media (especially Twitter, Facebook and Instagram for photos), in your prospectus, in advertisements, on posters at open days and more. These stories have a lifespan of a year or more so don't throw them away after Results Day.

8. Review and reflect

Once all the dust has cleared, it's always worth a few minutes making notes for next year or what worked and what didn't!

c) Experts

Schools contain experts on a number of issues. Your school will have teachers who are experts in their fields and may well have leaders who are experts on particular aspects of education, for example in use of technology or in education in a particular faith community. When this expertise is aligned with the key messages of the school, training and using the expert as a commentator will have a strong positive effect.

As an example, consider the role that Anthony Seldon[17] has played in promoting Wellington College. His historical scholarship and innovative thinking on education strongly support the school's image. Other head teachers such as Bernard Trafford of the Royal Grammar School Newcastle or Geoff Barton of King Edward VI School, Bury St Edmunds often write interesting and intelligent articles for their local newspapers.

How do you pick the right people? You need someone who can speak passionately yet concisely about the subject and who is highly flexible, something especially needed when dealing with journalists. They may require training in talking to the media, or in writing articles for the press. You need to write a short biography of the expert that makes it obvious why they are an expert, and have a high quality photograph available electronically.

Experts often have great contacts in their areas of expertise and should be encouraged to take opportunities to write or speak at conferences for example. The school marketing team can help arrange these events, and should be involved in writing articles and speeches. They should also publicise these events to other stakeholders.

---

[17] anthonyseldon.co.uk

In addition schools should look for opportunities for experts via their media relations programme – national and local media are often keen to talk to educationalists about their innovations and opinions.

d) Case studies

Case studies are not 'news' but they draw together information about individuals and teams to show how a school can meet the goals and ambitions set out in the key messages. In schools, case studies often focus on individual students and how the school has influenced and supported them to produce high achievement. Case studies can be of current students or recent alumni. They can however also look at successful and innovative departments, sports teams, teachers or clubs.

As with all evidence, choose case studies that have clear outcomes that support the key messages of the school. If your school is saying that it is highly academic, there should be profiles of high-achieving students. If the school is community-focused, examples of partnerships with local people should be prepared and used.

Creating a case study bank

A file full of case studies is a great asset for a school marketer. They can be used in a wide number of ways - in media relations, in prospectuses, on your website and in individual communications with parents. It is also good to use students who have been profiled as tour guides at events. They are proof of the impact your school has on individuals.

So, how do you set about creating your bank?

1. Identify the individuals to be profiled.

Even in a small school it's worth asking around - Heads of Year are a great place to start. Don't just ask for names - get teachers to say why the students demonstrate the key strengths of the school. Make sure you reflect the gender and ethnic mix of your school as well as the range of achievement in your school (don't just pick the academic or sporting heroes for example - look at those who help others or lead charity work especially if that is a key message). You should start with a list of 5-10 students - enough to give a decent range without taking too much time.

2. Obtain permission from parents.

Most schools routinely ask parents for permission to use their children in marketing activities, but it's worth sending a further permission letter home for a case study - many parents will also get a positive feeling from their child being singled out in this way!

3. Write a list of questions.

I always have a number of general questions that I ask every case study at a particular school. It means you don't miss out anything important - and you can cross-cut between questions in a video or prospectus.

Start with easy questions - how long they've been at the school, what they're studying, what they achieved in their GCSE exams or where they went to primary school for example. Then make sure to ask about the things that make your school different - what is it like studying in a Sixth Form College? Or a faith school? Or a single sex school? Then focus on their individual stories and achievements. What have they done at the school? How has it helped them to achieve? At this stage don't be too rigid when following the list - you can move away from your list and follow up any interesting statements they make.

4. Think multimedia when recording information.

Videoing case study interviews is a great idea. It allows you to focus on questioning rather than recording answers as well as giving access to video and audio material which can be put on your website or You Tube feed. More advice on capturing video is given later in this chapter.

5. Tag case studies and keep them up to date.

When you start writing case studies, you'll know your way around them. But as the bank increases it becomes more difficult to remember which was which. A simple filing system would list name, address, year group, exam results, extra-curricular activities referenced and date interviewed. Make sure to revisit case studies on at least an annual basis - and you can keep tracking students after leaving school of course!

6. Use them across different media over time.

While case studies may be generated initially for a prospectus or website, you should consider how to use them in all your marketing communications. One school I know puts out life-size cut-outs of case study students at Open Days - you could also show video clips at Parents' Evenings or add exam results to the case studies and sent them to local newspapers. They're also great for Direct Mail or newspaper adverts - you are telling prospective parents in their neighbourhood 'your child could be like this!

e) Research

Chapter 3 of the book has already covered market research. You can often communicate much of this research to stakeholders to improve their view of you – for example if it shows that perceptions of the school are changing for the better over time or that you are listening to the needs or parents and making changes in response.

However you can also do more general research to show that your school is interested in and understands key educational issues affecting its own students. An example of research would be a survey finding out the most important issues affecting children undergoing transition from primary to secondary education.

This would be genuinely interesting to parents, but could also be used to demonstrate specific innovations that your school carries out to help reduce problems caused by these issues.

If you are conducting research, make sure the research is conducted on a sufficiently large scale to make any statistical claims significant. Again, in many schools, Maths teachers are a great help with this!

f) Capturing stories in a multimedia world

When faced with the different communication methods described in the next chapter, it is important that stories are available in different formats. A story may form part of a written press release, may be shown as a video on your website or illustrated with powerful photographs in a school magazine - exciting stories such as top academic grades or raising a significant sum of money for charity will definitely appear in different media. News organisations such as the BBC and the Daily Telegraph[18] now operate multimedia newsrooms – you probably can't match that intensity in a school but the same principles can be applied!

The simplest way to ensure that you have multiple formats is to focus on video, recording everything on a good quality (HD capable) digital camcorder or camera, if possible using an external microphone and tripod. It is far easier to transcribe comments than to set up scenes for later videoing. Taking a series of still pictures with a digital camera will also help illustrate a story.

If a school trip is taking place, consider sending a student news team on the trip with a school video or still camera. Alternatively ask students and teachers to take pictures and email them to you. This could be incentivised through a photography competition!

It is also important to record detailed information about the people in the story and any dates or numbers referenced. In particular, you must take down names, ages and the general areas that people live in – local papers are far more willing to publicise the achievements of local people.

---

[18] www.youtube.com/watch?v=2yXT_1pvDv4&noredirect=1

When writing try to capture the whole story in the first paragraph and then give details sequentially so that the story can be easily cut down. Also make sure that stories are stored well as they can be used repeatedly for a number of months! Make sure to 'tag' them with details of the people involved, the key messages being communicated and key facts.

Once you have developed stories, you can also involve students in producing videos and writing media releases – again, very useful training for an aspiring journalist or marketing professional.

How to use video

The combination of cheap video cameras, fast video-editing software and social media means all schools can use video to communicate a wide range of messages! Here are a few basic tips, but if you do a lot of videoing you should consider going on a training course or using local experts.

Planning

1. Don't feel limited by video. Online platforms such as Vimeo and YouTube mean that you can add video to many types of communication – your website, a prospectus or newsletter, even an emailed invitation.

2. Wherever possible plan to let students communicate key messages in words or actions - don't spend too long on talking heads from senior management (even the Head!)

3. Brainstorm creative ideas for shots in advance but also be open to new ideas from those you are filming. Chemistry teachers often have some good ideas (I've filmed people having their hands set on fire and you can't fake those reactions!).

Shooting

4. Find a good but small HD video camera (and a small tripod) and

98

take it with you when following up any stories. You can transcribe a video and use the best bits later in a written prospectus, but you can't turn written notes into a video!

5. Try to use the best equipment for a major video - but don't worry if you're stuck with a camera phone if you see something newsworthy.

6. Don't make people stick to a script. The best video interviews are with people who know generally what they will be asked, but have flexibility to change their answers.

7. Take time - stop and reshoot if there are problems. Video cameras now have a lot of memory and it is usually obvious where you've edited clips! The downside is that videoing will ALWAYS take longer than you think.

Editing

8. Get help from others in the school if you're not that good at editing. Students and art teachers are often very good!

Sharing

9. Use social media such as YouTube and Vimeo to put videos on your website and share them via social media. Remember to show them at Open Days and any other suitable occasion!

g) How Whitefield Primary School embraced video

CASE STUDY from marketingadviceforschools.com

Sharing video is a great way of showcasing your school. Whitefield Primary School[19] in Liverpool has used video-sharing platform Vimeo extensively to show off the school. Videos are posted on the school website and shared in social media. The still below is from an excellent video that celebrates how the school develops a love of reading.

If you have a few minutes, I'd recommend looking around the school's website and seeing how effectively it uses a range of technology to communicate to parents and the wider community. And if you like any of the Vimeo videos, please share them yourself (just click on the paper airplane)!

Whitefield Primary School Vimeo video

---

[19] whitefieldprimary.co.uk

h) How to present data to parents and other stakeholders

Schools produce a lot of numbers - exam results, predicted grades, test results, value-added scores and more. Much data comes with complex acronyms - such as MIDYS, FFT, ALIS or ALPS. Teachers get to know the most important numbers - but how do you communicate this to parents and other stakeholders?

The most important things to do with any data are to SELECT, INTERPRET, PERSONALISE and PRESENT (SIPP).

1. Select

This does not mean just picking the most positive data and ignoring the rest! It means using data to back up the key messages and strengths of the school, as well as explaining honestly and practically any issues that you want to address.

Schools often overlook data that can support their key messages - for example I learned recently that one school has an excellent value added score for its less able students (and a pretty decent one for the more able!) but wasn't using it in marketing.

If you're not good with numbers, I suggest utilising your Head of Maths or Maths Co-ordinator - they'll love to extract and explain the data to you!

2. Interpret

Explain data in ways that parents and other non-specialist audiences can understand. Teachers understand what an Average Standardised Residual of +0.3 in ALIS means (good news), but parents need to know that it means A-level results were statistically above those to be expected from the intake!

Equally, parents may wonder why your VA score has dropped from 100.1 to 99.9 - you need to explain that these numbers are statistically the same (a graph showing change over a longer time period helps here!)

3. Personalise

This means showing what the data actually means for individuals (usually students) at the school. If 100% of students move up the expected number of levels from KS1 to KS2 (well done again!), use a case study or examples of their changing work to show how much they have learned.

If you've had a great A-level year, show how this has helped students achieve places in top universities.

4. Present

Many people looking at schools will not be that used to viewing data and presenting key data in a simple format will help them focus on the key issues. Consider using bar charts or pictograms to pick out key highlights online or in published documents.

At the same time, you need to be aware that you will have parents who will be very familiar with data analysis - so make sure you have raw data to back up any assertions and members of staff who can explain how your data has been presented.

i) Safeguarding issues

Working in a school, guarding the privacy and safety of students and other stakeholders is an important issue –but one that is made easier by preparing in advance.

The first important issue is that students under the age of 18 need active parental permission to take part in marketing activities. There are a wide number of reasons why a parent may not wish to have their child used in marketing and this needs to be strictly respected.

A school should deal with this in advance by sending a marketing permission form to parents when the student joins the school. If permission is not given, the names (not the reasons!) need to be shared with marketing staff. For a school starting up a marketing programme, this process may not have been in place and it is especially important to plan to obtain permission in advance of any filming.

If external journalists or other marketing experts are brought into a school, for example to speak to a news team, the marketing professional needs to be aware of the school's policy on visitors. In particular, if an expert (even a parent) is to work with students or to stay in school for a significant period of time they will need to undergo security checks and there will be the need for a risk assessment if they are bringing in additional equipment or if students are going off site.

The next issue that arises is use of student names and pictures in publicity. Local newspapers in particular use a range of techniques to avoid allowing readers to identify children. They may choose only to use first names in pictures, or to print full names but not to use address details as they would with adults. You should ensure that your school has an agreed policy that follows either of these routes.

A final issue is that of authority. Marketing staff will often be under pressure to send information to the media, but schools often require that senior leaders authorise any contact with the press. This is a good idea, but it will be important that this does not significantly slow down the process. Training a number of senior staff to authorise all but the most sensitive material and having material prepared in advance will significantly help here.

Chapter checklist...

- ☐ Are you able to find regular news stories from your school?
- ☐ Do you have you the capacity to produce a significant number of stories that cover all the key messages?
- ☐ Do you have the capability to produce video, audio and written news stories?
- ☐ Have you explored the idea of setting up a student news team to support your work?
- ☐ Have you identified case studies that show the impact of your school?
- ☐ Do you know how best to present data to external audiences?
- ☐ Are your marketing processes consistent with the safeguarding and data protection policies of the school?

CHAPTER SEVEN: USING MASS MEDIA

It seems a long way into the book to be hitting the areas that might have been traditionally thought of as marketing. However, by this point you now know what to communicate and to who – making the how much more likely to succeed!

There are a large number of communication tools explored in this chapter and the next one. This chapter focuses on mass media – the next on developing personal communications. The tools in this chapter are used to make key stakeholders aware of you and enable you to capture their personal details. In chapter 8 you can then communicate with them personally to develop stronger relationships.

a) Managing the marketing mix

How you mix these different media (sometimes known as the 'marketing mix') is a major challenge. You have a limited amount of money to spend and there will be many salespeople calling to offer their 'ideal' advertising or sponsorship opportunities.

The best way to handle this issue is to focus first on the essentials – you must have a website and some form of printed information for visitors – traditionally in the form of a prospectus. Beyond that, social media and media relations are the cheapest next steps provided you have time to create exciting and interesting copy and to manage journalist relationships and your Twitter and Facebook accounts.

Direct mail, sponsorship and advertising (on- or offline) are more expensive, while attending events may be a significant burden on your and colleagues' time, so you need to plan carefully and evaluate the impact your choices. Remember to refer back to research you have carried out before booking anything,

One of the more repetitive tasks in marketing is to carefully check all communications to ensure that the key messages and design are consistent across all communications and that there are no errors in any adverts or publications. In a school, you can reduce the effort by involving other staff. Invite teachers to proof publications and websites by posting copies on the staffroom noticeboard with some Post-It™ notes. Many teachers are good at finding small errors and will also suggest improvements to the design and other stories that you or your news team could follow up. There is nothing to be defensive about in this process – mistakes always happen in marketing and it is always better to have someone find a number of mistakes early in the design and advertising process.

Once you start the marketing programme, it is important to keep parents, staff and students on board by letting them know of new advertising campaigns, social media announcements or press coverage.

b) Your website

When Sir Tim Berners-Lee invented the World Wide Web, he gave organisations and individuals a unique gift – to present themselves as they would like to be seen to anyone in the world. Websites are now probably the most important part of any marketing programme. A survey by education consultants mtmconsulting[20] carried out in 2008 found that 94% of parents who researched schools said that they visited websites during the process – and in the intervening six years that number must now be approaching 100%. Unfortunately only 35% of parents described themselves as "very impressed" by the school websites they had visited.

The best schools websites are not the flashiest, busiest or most technologically advanced, but the ones that reinforce consistently the key messages the organisation want to put out, provide recent evidence that backs up the key messages, and give visitors the opportunity to find out more in a variety of ways.

Websites also have to work. Broken links and old web pages with the wrong information will cause visitors to give up searching or to become confused. If you have old information you should quickly update it or remove the page. One way of ensuring this is to encourage staff to check the website regularly and let you know of problems.

What should you have on your website? As seen above, putting too much information online can result in a lot of errors and a quickly out-of-date website. It is be best to focus on the essentials first:

- Key messages to quickly differentiate your school
- Contact information for the school – so that stakeholders can make personal contact – including email, telephone and address details.

---

[20] www.mtmconsulting.co.uk/insights/the-missing-million-report/

- A sign-up form for more information – you should try to gather basic information from prospects as soon as possible.
- Your news, case studies, expert commentary and research that support each key message (with an RSS or Twitter feed that can be subscribed to)
- Background information on the school (this will usually include the history of the school and details of the head teacher and other senior staff)
- Results of exams, OFSTED or ISI inspections
- Vacancies and information about working at the school
- Admissions information (including details of fees and bursaries for private schools)
- Calendar of events
- Information for current parents and/or students (these may be separate sites with links to educational material, student results and more)
- Other legal requirements (for example state schools need to supply the following:
    - Pupil Premium allocation, use and impact on attainment
    - Curriculum provision, content and approach, by academic year and by subject
    - Admission arrangements
    - The school's policy in relation to behaviour, charging, and SEN and disability provision
    - Links to Ofsted reports and to the Department's achievement and attainment performance data; and details of the school's latest Key Stage 2 and 4 attainment and progress measures.[21])

---

[21] 'Reducing bureaucracy in schools: Changes to school information regulations', www.education.gov.uk, 2012

It should be very easy for someone visiting your site to find what they want – many sites make it easier by giving each stakeholder (parent, prospective parent, jobseeker etc.) a specific part of the website, known as a 'landing page'.

While a complex design with animation and video may look appealing, in fact the best way to get people to find your site is to provide useful, well-organized, well-written, well-designed information, and to make sure that the website is the central communication point in all your other communications.

One interesting way of ensuring that content is up to date is to create one or more blogs. These could relate to news stories (the development of the new site), case studies ('my first few weeks in the Senior School') or experts ('how we're introducing a new way of teaching in Y7').

The more people who find your site and link to it, or send around the URL to their friends, the more visitors you'll have – and the higher the site will appear in search engines (see below). Word of mouth (or perhaps 'word of email') is very powerful on the Web!

It is perhaps best to separate the decisions around who creates a new website into two – initial design and ongoing changes. Most schools use an external designer to set up a website (although it is perfectly possible to do in-house), while most now maintain and update the site in-house through a content management system. If you are new to website design, talk to your IT team and a number of external experts before committing to any particular system.

A final thought – when you are setting up a website, make sure you are aware of how to track visitor numbers and the pages they visit yourself. This information is very powerful in working out which media are good at attracting visitors and which pages are most popular.

Keeping your website up to date

'Creating our school website was a challenge, but keeping it up to date is a chore!' is a common complaint from schools marketers. Here are 10 tips to make sure that visitors to your school site get the latest and best information!

1. Make sure you have an effective content management system (CMS) that you can use yourself - it is far more efficient than emailing content to an external agency or IT expert. CMSs are now very easy to understand and work on similar principles to desktop publishing programmes. Make sure that as many staff as possible (and certainly more than one) are trained up and regularly post content.

2. Make the approval process as simple as possible. While you should always get a second opinion before posting anything (to check spelling and grammar as well as content), you don't need the Head and/or the Chairman of Governors to look at all content before it is posted.

3. Make the website the centre of your marketing activity - put all news stories and events on the site first so that you're not having to duplicate content from elsewhere.

4. Divide the site into different areas with different deadlines. Some parts may need updating on a weekly basis (e.g. news, job vacancies); some on a termly basis (e.g. list of teaching staff, calendar of events); and others should be checked on an annual basis, ideally in the summer holidays (e.g. exam results, admissions arrangements, pupil premium information).

5. Assign clear responsibility for each section with deadlines. If you need updates from other members of staff, makes sure they know when and how to put them on the website (or who to send them to).

6. Involve other staff and hold regular editorial meetings. Not only is this a great way of generating new story ideas, it gives you a regular check on progress.

7. Remove out of date material as soon as possible. Some CMSs allow you to automatically archive material - very useful for blog posts and event warnings.

8. Encourage feedback and contributions. Ask people (students, parents, governors) to let you know if there is anything out of date - and to contribute stories, photographs of their activities. Don't see feedback like this as a criticism!

9. Resist the temptation to add more pages to your website. Try to always fit new content into the existing structure - new pages can be forgotten about and give an out-of-date impression of the school.

10. Try new ideas to keep you interested. Set up a blog, create a video diary for an expedition, set up a Twitter feed using your news content - something that will keep you (and others) coming back to the website.

c) Search Engines

According to research by Pew, in January 2002, 52% of all Americans used search engines. In February 2012 that figure had grown to 73%. On any given day in early 2012, more than half of American adults using the internet used a search engine (59%)[22]. The UK might slightly lag behind the USA, but it seems clear that if someone is not aware of your school's website address, or is looking generally for relevant schools, they will use search engines. And that means your school needs to score highly in Google, Bing and Yahoo!'s rankings. How can you ensure this?

When you use most search engines you will see two lists – a list of the most relevant websites as assessed by the search engine, plus a series of adverts that people have paid to place against the key words you used in the search.

Optimising Your Site

Appearing high up in the search engine list comes from having a website that closely meets the search criteria and contains relevant content. The practice of improving your position in this search is called 'search engine optimisation' (SEO).

You can check how well your website is doing by coming up with a list of key phrases that parents and other stakeholders would use to find a school - for example 'private schools in Dorset' or 'Catholic primary schools in Newcastle' and entering these into the search engines of a computer or mobile phone (if you have a Google+ account make sure you log out of this before using Google as a search engine as your own browsing history, which is likely to include your own school website, will be taken into account). If your site does not appear on the first

---

[22] pewinternet.org/Reports/2012/Search-Engine-Use-2012/Summary-of-findings.aspx

page, or competitor schools appear above you, you should take steps to improve your ranking.

You should first check (or ask your web designer to check) whether the right search terms are written into the code of the front page of your site (the 'metatags') and that your site is registered with Google and Bing. You should also make sure that the important search terms are on the front page of your website, are used in articles you put up on your website, and that your site is updated regularly.

For advice on further improving your ranking (the criteria used by search engines change on a regular basis) it is best to contact an expert in SEO and ask for their advice (it might be a good idea to search for a local expert online!).

Advertising in Search Engines

To appear high up in the advertising list, you need to invest in the search engine's advertising programme – the best known is Google AdWords[23] but you could also try Yahoo! Advertising[24]. Each system has good user guides and will take you stepwise through the process of choosing key words and placing a value on each 'click-through' you get.

If you are investing in search engine advertising, take it slowly at first and make sure you evaluate success as you can spend a lot of money quickly! It is also important that the 'landing page' that the searcher finds first on your website is relevant to their enquiry and has a sign up form for more information. This means that you can tie your advertising spend directly to new leads.

---

[23] *adwords.google.co.uk*

[24] advertising.yahoo.com

d) Social Media and the wider Internet

The same Internet that allows you to post your website allows others to post their opinions on anything that matters to them. They can do this to selected 'friends' through networks such as Facebook[25] or to the whole world through website discussion forums or open access channels such as Twitter[26]. While there is a wide variation in use of social media, schools need to be aware of the benefits and dangers this brings.

A survey of 25 UK schools that Marketing Advice for Schools carried out in 2013 showed that all schools are taking on social media, but there are interesting differences between sectors, in particular the use of Facebook.

Across all schools, Facebook is the most popular platform (80%), followed by Twitter (68%). The third most popular is LinkedIn, with 24% of the schools surveyed making use of the professional networking site. Other platforms were less popular with only 16% on Google+, 12% on Pinterest and 8% on Instagram.

Facebook use varies widely though - 100% of Independent schools and 90% of Free Schools and Academies use the platform, compared to only 20% of those in Local Authority control. By contrast, Twitter is used by 80% of all state schools (LA/Free Schools/Academies) but only 56% of Independent schools.

Social media can be divided into three main areas:

---

[25] www.facebook.com

[26] www.twitter.com

Closed networks e.g. Facebook, LinkedIn, or Instagram: These allow people to post comments, photographs and personal information and share it with their contacts. While this information can be shared wider, the majority of users communicate with their contacts.

A school can set up a presence on these sites to enable its stakeholders to talk to each other and to find out information about the school. For example Facebook is increasingly a place to set up alumni networks, while LinkedIn[27] allows you to develop a shared area for staff development and recruitment.

Open networks e.g. Twitter: These networks are more focused on general communication. For example micro-blogging site Twitter allows users to send short 'tweets' that can be searched by anyone. Schools should consider setting up a Twitter feed to make announcements of news stories, events and website updates. It is important that the account is used regularly but that its use is monitored and that it is not used to send anything unprofessional.

Internet forums: Perhaps overlooked a little, discussion sites contain ongoing discussions on educational issues. Sites such as MumsNet[28] (and its competitor NetMums[29]) allow parents to give positive and negative comments on individual schools. It is useful to identify which online forums are used by your stakeholders and to monitor comments – if a comment is derogatory or unfair you can take action to correct or remove comments. You may also contemplate advertising on these sites if your market research shows many prospective parents using them.

---

[27] linkedin.com

[28] mumsnet.com

[29] netmums.com

Starting with Social Media

1. Get current students and parents to help you with your research.

You should always be aware of which social media are being used by your key stakeholder groups. Take every opportunity to ask students and parents which social media they use. You can also ask a group of parents or trusted students to research your school and let you know what is being said about it, perhaps as part of an IT project.

2. Work on content based marketing

Write stories that say good things about the school that can be used across different media, rather than writing just for the website or a prospectus.

3. Record everything in multimedia

Don't just write a story, take pictures and videos. Instagram and Pinterest rely heavily on photos, YouTube on videos. Encourage students to write, blog or photograph events and send you their contributions.

4. Let (and encourage) parents, students and other stakeholders to put stories on their social media.

You can easily put photos up and let students share them on Instagram or videos on You Tube. A couple of examples of educational institutions that have set up news pages on their websites to enable this (suggested by US marketer Steve Momorella - thanks!) are newsroom.hacc.edu and oxfordschools.org.

5. Monitor social media

You need to know what people are saying about your school by tracking online content. If you find negative comments, don't react badly – you need to politely reply if the facts are wrong, and work to change perceptions if you are seen in a bad light. If you come across students behaving badly you should swiftly apply appropriate sanctions in your school's IT policy.

e) How Bablake School uses social media to develop communities

CASE STUDY from marketingadviceforschools.com

Bablake School was the top school in the 2013 Interactive Schools 'UK Independent Schools Social Media Influence' league table. *Marketing Advice for Schools* caught up with *Mark Woodward, Webmaster (and Head of Careers) at Bablake* to find out how the school had embraced social media and the impact it has had on the school.

Mark has had an interesting career path. He started off as a Classics teacher, then took over responsibility for careers education. In 2006 he stopped teaching and as well as careers education took over responsibility for the school website and publications. Mark had been using the Internet for careers research for a while and had set up his own careers website to help students access careers information (www.woodyswebwatch.com - worth a visit in itself!). He was aware that students were going online for careers information and started to educate them in safe use of the Internet.

His work led in a logical progression to setting up social media. The first step was to work with his Headmaster and Director of Studies on a general policy. They didn't find any obvious problems with setting up a Twitter account but were much more tentative about Facebook given the less open nature of the platform. However, the students and parents were keen and so Mark worked with two of the school's senior prefects to draw up a proposal for moderating the school Facebook page. All posts are moderated, but there has been little problem in reality, Mark commenting 'people know you can't be anonymous'. Having said that, he would also be able to identify issues affecting the school and pass them on to senior management to address quickly if something critical happened.

The school now has a flexible approach to social media - they know that different groups will use different media. Facebook is used mainly by 25-35 year old former pupils, but they are seen as very important as they have their own families and become parents of the next generation of potential students. Students at the school favour newer social media - Instagram and Snapchat are popular. The school tries new platforms and moves on if they're not seen to have a significant take-up - 'we've tried Tumblr and Google+ but they weren't popular - we're now looking at Vine', adds Mark.

What links the different social media is a central approach to content development. Mark gets content from across the school - from staff, the school diary and from the other school publications he edits. He has started using WhatsApp to get content from teachers leading school trips.

He produces one key story per day during term time as well as 60 stories to use across the holidays, but will also focus more time on the biggest stories - for example the school recently worked with a school in South Africa to offer a range of practical help, including creating the school's website. He is keen to post the stories in real time wherever possible in order to be able to reply to the wider community, although he does admit to occasionally scheduling website posts in the long holidays if likely to be away from a Wi-Fi connection.

Mark believes that the school's success comes from having an insider working on communications - "I'm part of a group of local private schools and some have outsourced social media - that means that content is regularly posted but there's no interaction. My goal is to 'make it real' and show that we are the best school in the Midlands.' Mark is also able to approach staff as a peer and for example offer advice on the best photographs to take.

What is the impact? In numerical terms there are a lot of people engaging with the school - the school has almost 2,000 Twitter followers and over 1,000 followers on the school's main Facebook page and over 700 on the Alumni page. They are also active - with typically 500 Facebook visitors per day and a highly active Twitter community that includes celebrities and many former students. The school has managed to weather the economic downturn well, but Mark says that the biggest impact has been in relationship development - 'for example we've had former students come back to give advice to current students'.

Bablake School at night

f) Publications

It is important to have a publication that visitors can take away and read after visiting you or that you can send out on request to the shrinking number of people who don't prefer to look at websites. The majority of schools produce one or more prospectuses on an annual basis to meet this need. While this does work for many school it's important to realise that there are cheaper and perhaps more effective alternatives.

One alternatively is to create a school folder and a series of inserts covering the key messages you want to communicate. This allows the publication to be personalised as well as easily updated for example with new case studies or news such as an OFSTED inspection or exam results. It is also much cheaper than throwing away many copies of last year's prospectus!

An alternative idea used by some schools is to reverse the focus above and produce a 'school yearbook' with the sort of information used in a prospectus added as an insert instead. This uses the news stories and case studies from the year, and often adds in exemplary material from students – whether creative writing, extended project work or art work.

Whichever publication you choose, as with the school website, it must enable those reading it to make contact with the school and contain email and telephone contact details. It should also be circulated to staff and other stakeholders so that they can refer to the correct information when talking to prospective parents. You should also investigate the various ways of putting every publication onto your website – either as a downloadable document or as an online publication that can be browsed directly.

How can you make sure that your prospectus is read and helps sell your school? Here are some tips to help you...

1. Identify the messages you want to get across.

Your prospectus needs to quickly highlight the key strengths that make your school different. It also needs to be consistent with all the other advertising that stakeholders see.

2. Use stories to back up every statement.

It is easy to say that your school is academic, or caring, or hi-tech. It is much more important to demonstrate what this means to students at the school. You should use case studies of students, hard evidence such as exam grades, awards, or value added performance, and external endorsements from parents, OFSTED or the ISI wherever possible. If you say you offer small class sizes or great pastoral care, give evidence!

3. Let your students illustrate the prospectus.

Don't just put the same picture of the front of your school on the prospectus – parents will be able to see this! Ask students to draw, paint or design their image of the school or to choose photographs that show what the school means to them. You can also include exemplary student material inside the document – whether this is creative writing, a scientific poster, or the sheet music of a new composition. If you use pictures of sporting or drama events, identify the event.

4. Use a folder to make it easy to update.

In the world of weekly website updates and daily Twitter feeds, you need to be able to add information to your prospectus more than once a year. Swapping your printed booklet for a colour folder with space for updates is a simple solution that saves a lot of money.

5. Personalise your prospectus.

When you meet parents, let them tell you what is most important to them. At the end of their visit, tour or event give them a personal prospectus with the most relevant case studies and information. A handwritten note also generates amazing goodwill!

6. Give lots of contact details.

Your prospectus must of course contain websites, phone numbers and email addresses of key people, but you could also set up specific Twitter feeds and Facebook pages for prospective parents.

7. Add in the latest news and details of future events

Using a folder will also allow you to slip in details of forthcoming sporting events, concerts and other events that show your school off.

8. Don't ration or hide them.

Some schools I know take the view that prospectuses are too valuable to hand out to anyone who isn't a serious applicant. My response to that is that in the overall context of a school's marketing budget, prospectuses are relatively cheap (and if they're not, use some of the tips above to reduce the costs!). More importantly a prospectus may be passed around a number of families and friends so please put enough out at events for current parents, teachers, governors and other contacts to take them.

9. Let your staff see them

There's nothing more embarrassing and likely to lead to problems at Open Days than if prospective parents know more about the school than teachers appear to. Please take time to talk all staff who come into contact with prospective and current parents through each new prospectus – paying particular attention to the stories and facts that back up your school's key messages (and get them to add their own!)

g) Advertising

You can place an advert in many places including newspapers, magazines, websites, radio, television, advertising hoardings, public transport, sports grounds and in buildings used by various communities, and on your own buildings!

Advertising usually involves paying twice – once to design the advert in whatever form it appears (print, audio, video) plus once to rent the advertising space. Essentially you are paying one party to create a compelling message and another party to directly put your message to potential customers.

Because you are paying for an advert, you have a high degree of control over your messages when compared say to media relations, but you also need to carefully manage your budget and evaluate which advertising options make sense. You must match spending to the needs of the school and be sure that you make your budget last - don't spend all your money straight away and be left with no money to publicise your last Open Event or admission deadline.

Advertising starts with research. If market research has been carried out with stakeholders you will have a good idea of which publications, websites and other media they read and watch. Ask teachers and current parents where they would look for information about schools and ask newsagents which local papers are popular. There are also guidebooks such as the Good Schools Guide which are very influential for some parents, as well as a host of free magazines aimed at parents and distributed door-to-door or via shops and schools.

Once you have a list of possible places to advertise, look at them carefully and research which organisations are advertising in them. Call the advertising departments of the publications and ask for a media pack – information about the publication which should include typical costs of advertising and information about the readership.

In a larger school with a significant marketing budget, it is worth talking to advertising agencies. They will often manage the whole advertising process including creative design, research and media buying. Agencies make money by negotiating discounts with advertisers so can be very useful for media buying in particular.

You should then move on to consider the design of your advert. Whether you are producing this in-house or using the help of an advertising or design agency, all adverts need to use the key messages, evidence, and design guidelines you have agreed above. The easiest way I've found to make your advert different from other schools is to use real-life examples and quotes – too many schools just use adverts to announce events, rather than to say why a parent should attend them.

You should be flexible in adding additional information to reflect the readership of the publication and the latest news from your school. For example it makes a lot of sense to include case study information that relates to the area the publication circulates in.

The next step is to work out an advertising timetable. Make sure that you talk to the media or your advertising agency regularly and well in advance of any deadlines to see exactly what they need – late booking fees and changes of design can be expensive. You need to build in time for checking and proofreading – it is embarrassing if a school has spelling mistakes in its adverts or if the telephone number is wrong! Make sure that people seeing the advert have a number of ways to respond.

For any media, talk to the advertising executives and listen to any ideas that they have for increasing your impact. You could for example explore the opportunity to place 'advertorials' or 'advertising features' in written media. These are paid for articles that allow you to give more information about your school and to use the case studies and news stories you have built up, but they will not be trusted to the same extent as a piece of media coverage. The advantage is that you get full control over the copy and illustration. You could also look to advertise in print and online versions of a publication or just online. If you are advertising on radio, explore the idea of sponsoring a specific show that your target audience might listen to.

Publications can be imaginative in offering different ways of advertising – from advertising on covers to combined online and offline packages. When evaluating different ways of advertising, it often helps to create a mock-up of the advert in the same position in the publication or webpage and see if you or others notice the advert when reading. This process will also help you if you have a choice of page for advertising – remember that right-hand pages are seen more often! You should also not be frightened to ask for discounts, especially if you are advertising for the first time in a publication or in a new publication.

Once you have an agreed and printed advert, as well as placing it in paid-for media, look for places to advertise for free – for example in feeder schools, places of worship or shops owned by parents or governors. You can also give copies of advertising material to teachers, parents and governors and ask them to put them up in such locations or put them up in the staff room.

Finally, don't miss the opportunity to advertise on the outside of your school buildings! Banners are relatively cheap and remind passers-by and parents of forthcoming events.

h) Direct Mail, Email and Telephone

Direct mailshots cut out the 'middleman' of advertising – you deliver your advert directly to potential customers, whether physically in their mailbox, online or to their telephone. These techniques are not always welcomed by recipients and it is important to respect their wishes about future contact, but in a targeted way they can be very successful.

In written direct mail there are two stages, as in advertising. You produce the material you want to send and then find a cost-effective way to identify the target audience and send the material. Written direct mail usually has a strong 'call to action' – asking the recipient to call, visit a website or visit a school for an event – in order to check whether the mailshot has worked.

A paper mailshot usually consists of a letter as well as an advert or other advertising material – as people expect letters through the post! An e-mail mailshot usually consists of text and images with a link to a website for further information (don't include attachments as these are often rejected by anti-spam programs). As with advertising there are a number of external agencies that can advise on all stages of the operation. They can use sophisticated software to identify for example the streets in your area that are likely to have parents who can afford private education. Alternatively a primary school with a small catchment area could arrange for material to be posted through all the relevant local doors by volunteers!

Email can be used at this stage, but unless you have permission to send it you are likely to find much ends up being treated as unwanted 'spam'. That why I've left it to the next chapter to explain more about how to best use mass email – sending personalised newsletters to those who have given you permission.

Telephone calling is relatively rare when calling prospective parents, but it has been used a lot recently in the UK to keep in touch with schools and university alumni networks – perhaps something for more schools to try in the future (with the correct training and safeguards or course!).

i) Media relations

Media relations is the art of achieving positive coverage in newspapers, radio, television and increasingly online media including websites and social media. The value of media coverage is that people are more likely to believe and respond to positive messages in a publication they trust than in an advertisement. Media coverage also has the advantage of being free, but requires a significant amount of work. (By the way, if a publication asks for money in exchange for coverage, you should consider this as advertising, not media relations – the quality of your news is less important in this case than your bank balance!).

Media relations is often presented as a matter or writing and sending press releases, but this is not the best way to get media coverage for a school. It is possible to buy a media database, write press releases and send them out to hundreds of publications in seconds, then sit back and count the mentions in secondary and peripheral media, but the best coverage comes from tailored approaches to the key media that matter.

Journalists get the vast majorities of stories from press officers and other PR professionals. They know that they have to build up good relationships with them. But they dislike 'PRs' who have done no research, and have no idea what their publication covers or whether a press release is relevant or not. They might not run your story, but they will be much more amenable (and likely to talk to you in future) if your news is personalised, targeted and reasonable. If it has a good 'hook' and is well written they will like you even more.

Treat journalists as you would parents or other important customers. Make notes on what they like, which areas they cover, when they like to receive material, when they are on their final deadline (NEVER talk to a journalist 'on deadline' if you can help it), even what sports they like. You must keep a record of every contact you make. Journalists do make mistakes but if the mistake is unimportant don't mention it and if it is don't threaten them - most publications will make corrections if approached in a polite way.

In most publications there is a big difference between NEWS and FEATURES. Features are planned and written well in advance. Newspapers and magazines will publish schedules of features in many areas because they want businesses to advertise in these areas. Talk to advertisers to find out what is planned and who the commissioning editors are. Then get in early, suggest ideas to journalists, be friendly, and offer high quality photos.

Local papers will typically plan regular education features. It may take a year or so to get in sync with these - so don't panic if you miss things early on.

News stories are not planned - each day/week/month editors will discuss ideas and assign journalists to follow up stories. That doesn't mean you can't suggest stories in advance. If you have an exciting visitor planned, let the press know early so they can put in in a forward planning diary. Other news stores are reactive – journalists will want expert comment for example on changes to school curricula. That's where prepared and available expert commentators and emailing quick sound bite comments come in.

If you have a story that is not time-sensitive, try to fit it to the timescale of the most important media target. The 'exclusive' is one of the least true statements in the media, but journalists like getting a scoop. 'Embargoes' (where you put a time that a story can be used from at the top of the news release) do exist but unless you have a specific reason for using one (such as disclosing financial results in a stock market listed company or sending out the content of a speech in advance) you don't really need them.

Use materials you've prepared earlier to help you. Photographs, case studies and biographies of experts all help journalists write stories more easily.

How does this work in practice? For example, when your GCSE or A-level results day approaches, don't wait and send a press release on the day. Prepare case studies that you can drop results into in advance.

Choose interesting examples with strong 'hooks' (do you have twins or triplets getting results? Is there an example of a student who has overcome a difficulty in their personal life?).

A few weeks before the results day, let local journalists know when your results will be available and ask if they would be interested in visiting the school or in having comments and photographs emailed to them.

Once you know the results, ask students who have done well to give quotes and interviews. Take photographs and videos and write up your own news stories as well!

Over time you will build up good relationships with local media, but if you need to move more quickly, media relations (or public relations) consultancies might be a good choice. You need to pick an expert that has a strong relationships with your local media and experience of working with education if at all possible.

Negative media attention

Schools can sometimes worry about getting involved with the media, because of their role in reporting bad news. However, the best antidote to bad news in the media about a school is good news in the same media, and good relationships with local journalists can help when something does go wrong at a school.

But what should you do when something does go wrong? Schools do face crises following from issues such as allegations of abuse or tragic incidents involving current or former students or members of staff.

The key to handling a crisis is to plan ahead and having an agreed policy – you won't know what form the crisis will take, but there are key steps to take in all situations. These include consulting key individuals (including Governors) before issuing any statements to the press, ensuring that all stakeholders groups are considered so that for example parents don't hear about issues directly from the press. In the majority of cases, taking expert advice from your local authority or a specialist crisis management agency should be the first step.

In the longer term, the best way to recover from the negative impression people will get from a crisis is to keep communicating the key messages that make your school different – you need to keep moving on with your core marketing strategy and realise that crises will pass.

j) Sponsorship

Sponsorship covers a wide range of activities where a school gives money, time, expertise or physical space to a partner organisation to help promote both parties. Examples would include organising or financing competitive sports teams (of any standard from a competition between feeder primary schools to local professional teams), arranging a lecture series, hosting a careers fair for local schools, running an essay, poetry or debating competition, or holding events to support a local or national charity.

Successful sponsorship involves a genuine partnership where the sponsor adds more than just money, and where the outcome of the activity demonstrates one or more of the key messages of the sponsoring organisation. For example a school that is positioning itself as academic would benefit more from sponsoring a lecture series than one looking to be seen as community-friendly or successful at sport. It is important to realise that money does not always need to change hands – for example major sporting organisations often work with schools to improve their local awareness and make new fans.

Given the wide range of potential 'sponsorships', where do you start? The first place is to look at the existing relationships you have in place and see how they can be developed further – for example all schools raise a lot of money for charity but many do this in an unorganised way with different year groups and classes supporting different causes. Focusing on supporting one charity with a major event such as a 'Run for Life' will almost certainly allow more money to be raised and more publicity for both the school and the charity.

You can then look to targeted sponsorship of events that are of interest to your target audience. As with advertising remember to negotiate to make the most of your partnership – for example if you are sponsoring a sporting competition, can you offer reduced price tickets to students and parents? Could some of your students be mascots?

k) Exhibitions and Fairs

The final way of meeting prospective parents and getting your school noticed by other stakeholders is to attend exhibitions and fairs organised by third parties. These range from small village fêtes which will attract a wide selection of a local community to dedicated school events such as the Independent Schools Shows[30] that take place in London and other global cities.

As with other marketing activities it is very important to think carefully about which events you attend, what you do at them, and how you will evaluate success or failure afterwards. Here are three issues to focus on:

1. Cost

The cost of attending an event is not just what you pay for your stall or stand. Remember to factor in the time of those exhibiting, the costs of materials (and often food!) you are giving away and any 'extras' such as advertisements in an exhibition brochure.

2. Location

Your position within an exhibition is vital – if you are away from the main attractions and the entrances you will get few visitors. Make sure that you carefully consider where you will be exhibiting – the best way to get a good choice of locations is to book early and make sure to confirm exactly where your stand or stall will be.

3. Your wider contribution to the event

Taking a stall at a fair is just one way of showing off your school. As with sponsorship, think carefully about how to maximise your presence. If a school show has a programme of talks, can you put up

---

[30] schoolsshow.co.uk

an expert to help parents through issues such as the school application process or (for private schools) different ways of paying for schools? Could your school provide musicians or a dance troupe for a village fete?

Chapter checklist...

- ☐ Have you evaluated the key media you need to use against the budget available?
- ☐ Do you have a comprehensive, updated and consistent website?
- ☐ Do you have a flexible school publication that uses the content you have produced already?
- ☐ Have you considered conducting mailshots or e-mailshots to key stakeholder groups?
- ☐ Have you checked where your school ranks in the major internet search engines?
- ☐ Have you considered the advantages of social media?
- ☐ Have you a systematic advertising plan for media that you know your stakeholders read?
- ☐ Have you given advertising material to parents, students, staff and governors to pass around the local community?
- ☐ Have you identified the key journalists who write about education stories in your key media?
- ☐ Do you have a media relations plan that informs key media in advance of news stories?
- ☐ Do you have a crisis plan that includes how to deal with media enquiries?
- ☐ Have you considered lending your school's premises or expertise to support other organisations?
- ☐ Do you and others check all marketing materials for consistency and accuracy?

CHAPTER EIGHT: RELATIONSHIP MANAGEMENT

Using the tactics in the previous chapter will mean that key stakeholders are aware of your school and interested enough to give you their personal details. You now need to build up a picture of what they want from the school and communicate with them to meet these needs.

a) Making the first contact last (Awareness to Interest)

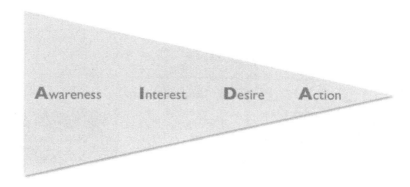

One of the best known marketing acronyms is AIDA - E St Elmo Lewis' famous model of how customers buy - often called the 'Marketing Funnel' today. While there are a host of later developments (and challenges to the idea itself!), I like the simplicity of the idea. Customers first become Aware of a product or service, then show Interest, then Desire and finally take Action. This means you have to take actions at each stage to move a prospective parent on.

Whether the first contact someone makes is via the telephone, an email, a personal meeting with a teacher or attendance at an event, it starts a parent thinking about what the experience their child will have. The contact must be positive, welcoming and friendly. If the parent phones in, there should be someone able to take the call or at the very least to return the call within a few minutes. If an email is sent, it must get to the right person to answer quickly. At an event, a new face must be greeted quickly.

However friendly and positive the initial contact is, it is vital for an organisation to gather information to allow further contact and to work out which marketing spend works. You must not assume that because someone is friendly and positive that they will attend the Open Day you discussed, or that they will visit the website as you suggested. You need to be able to remind them!

In order of priority, here are the key things to obtain from a new contact. It often helps to print contact forms for receptionists and others who may answer phone calls – one innovative company put these questions on mouse mats for customer-facing staff. If the meeting is face-to-face, it is important that the person meeting the prospect asks these questions and is able to write it down as soon as possible.

1. Name and salutation (it can be embarrassing if you get this wrong!)

2. Contact details – email, address and phone number as a minimum – and how they would prefer to be contacted.

3. Reason for calling in as much detail as possible. In the context of a prospective parent you need to find out which children are they calling about, how old are they and which school do they currently go to at a minimum.

4. Why they are calling – is it in response to an advert or media coverage (and which one!), through word-of-mouth (and who recommended them) or due to an existing relationship.

5. What they want from the school now? Do they want to visit, do they want a prospectus, or do they want to book a place on an Open Day?

6. What is it about the school that attracted them and made them call? If a prospective parent, what do they want most in a school for their child or children?

7. Any timeline that they are working on. Do they need to find a school for the start of the next academic year or are they moving for some reason before then?

8. Any other information. Are there specific interests they or their children have? Did they mention what they would like to see in the school they choose? For fee-paying schools, did they mention fees or bursaries?

9. Permission to send further material. It is not always easy to ask this question but it is important that you ask permission, especially if you send e-mails with information.

Once someone has made contact with your school it is important that you respond quickly to them with the information they need and in the way that they prefer. If you take a week to get back to them they will be less positive!

As well as sending the information requested, it helps to add a personal touch. A quick handwritten note on a cover slip or letter will give a positive impression and communication from a senior member of staff (even their email address) will be more effective than an unsigned letter or email from an 'admin' email address!

You then need to follow up this first contact. Make a note to call 3 days later and make sure that you talk to the person. Ask them for their views on the material you have sent them and if there is anything else they need to know about. Then invite them to visit!

b) Standing out from the crowd (Interest to Desire)

By getting parents to a come on a visit to your school, you've got their Interest, although they will also be showing interest in a number of other schools. How do you create the Desire that will lead to Action (the application to join?).

A parent's first visit to a school will usually either be for a personal visit or an Open Event. Some school marketers, especially in the private sector, are becoming sceptical about using Open Events and strongly favour personal visits. However, individual visits would be impracticable for highly oversubscribed state schools, which nevertheless still need people to choose them! I've therefore split the process of creating Desire into two – follow the first article if you use personal visits and the second if you run Open Events.

A. Visits

The aim of a personal visit is to reinforce the key messages about the school as well as to find and answer any questions that may be worrying the prospective parent. Here are four top tips to help this.

1. Use the information you already have

The visitor should ideally be met by the person who has talked to them before the visit and then introduced to the senior member of staff who is leading the visit - in any case the notes taken before the visit need to be shared with those involved in the visit. Always use student guides to help with the tour – it makes sense to tell them a little about the background of the visitor (be careful not to share confidential details).

2. Make a real effort to obtain full feedback from prospective parents, including any reservations.

Parents often have a high level of deference to teachers and especially head teachers based on their school experience and may be unwilling to express negative opinions. If you find any problems, take action to resolve them as soon as possible by finding the best expert in the school (for example a Head of Year for pastoral or medical concerns, or the Bursar for funding issues).

3. Don't try to put on a show or follow a script

Parents want to see the school as it is and if asked would really want to talk to current students and ask them about their views of the school rather than a member of senior management!

4. Follow up the visit with a personal reply

The best way of following up a visit is a personal phone call, letter or email that addresses any issues that came up during the visit and reinforces the key messages of the school.

B. Open Events

Making the most of Open Days

Open Days are incredibly important for any school – you have a captive audience of people who are interested in your school. Your goal is to make sure that they leave wanting to take the relationship further and apply.

When I moved into teaching I was interested to see how schools planned and ran these, given my experience of organising trade exhibitions in a previous working life. I found a lot of variation, some really hard work, but never enough planning! I think that many schools could benefit from some of the steps below:

1. Link Open Days to your marketing plan

Think carefully about what you are looking to communicate to prospective parents and students – focus on your strengths, innovations and positive recent stories. Make sure you can back up anything you put in an advert! Given the competition schools are now facing, it is definitely worth learning what other schools are saying about themselves as well.

2. Show student achievements off in as many ways as possible

You can present case studies as videos, as posters, or as presentations from the students themselves. Ask the students to help make these. Highlight the strengths of the school that differentiate yourself from others.

3. Use current parents to sell as well as students and teachers

I've never seen the PTA used to do more than pour drinks or sell uniform. Let them talk privately to prospective parents or ask some to present on how they have found the school!

4. Make sure everyone knows what to say

Few teachers are briefed properly before an Open Day – something that would scare any commercial exhibitor to death! All teachers, students and parents involved should have copies of information given to visitors in advance, know what the strengths of the schools are and who parents and prospective students should be directed to answer any difficult questions.

5. Try to make the event less rushed and formal

Don't make the head teacher give the same formal speech again and again – show a short video on a loop and use the time to let them talk to every parent individually or as a small group. This also means less of a crush in the school hall!

6. Involve visitors in the process

Don't just take visitors on a tour – give them short bursts of actual lessons (parents and potential students!), create a treasure hunt, let them make something to take home, write a communal story or poem or make a sculpture together.

7. Personalise the event

If you know someone who speaks a particular language or comes from a particular ethnic group is coming along, match them with similar current students. If you know a parent is particularly interested in sporting facilities or a particular subject, make sure you send them there first.

8. Walk in your visitors' shoes

Think about what a parent or student wants to see and plan a route to make it easy for them to do this. Make sure you walk the route they will be taking and check you see the right messages and the right people. And you don't have to show them the whole school!

9. Make sure you know who attended

Get everyone to fill in a feedback form and check their details against people who you thought were going to attend. Make sure you contact anyone who didn't make it and invite them to another event or for a personal tour. Ask teachers and students for specific feedback as well - make it easy for them with a simple shared spreadsheet or paper form.

10. Don't leave any questions unanswered

If anyone asks a teacher, student or parent a difficult questions, the visitor needs to be passed on to someone who can help. If this can't be done, take contact details and make sure a follow up call or email takes place.

11. Follow the Open Day up

A day or two after the event, email as many people as possible with outcomes from the event (pictures, your collective story, details of who attended) – and an invitation to other events (concerts, sporting fixtures, etc.) or a personal tour of the school. You can also share highlights via Twitter, Facebook, Instagram or other social media.

12. Reflect on each Open Day as it happens

As soon as possible, get a sample of those involved together to find out what was good and what needed improving!

c) Don't ever stop marketing! (Desire to Action)

Don't ever assume you've 'landed' a customer until their child starts at school - and of course that's when the even more important task of delivering an excellent education starts!

It's a great feeling when a parent agrees to send their child to your school - whether this is through a formal admissions process administered by the Local Authority or directly in the case of a private school. However, that shouldn't be the end of the process. You need to keep in touch with them for a wide range of reasons - to create a sense of excitement to ensure they turn up (especially if you don't have a huge waiting list!), to spread the word about your school in their communities, and importantly to make sure they tell you of any concerns or issues!

Here are the key ways to do this...

1. Ask them what they're interested in.

When you send out acceptance letters, ask the parents what their interests are and how they'd like to hear from the school. Ask for email and mobile phone details, and also encourage them to follow your school on social media such as Facebook and Twitter.

2. Give them people to talk to.

Make sure that your initial information contains details of people to ask questions of. This should include the person responsible for admissions at the school, but also a PTA contact (you could have local representatives) and the teacher who is responsible for the year group.

3. Create a dedicated 'new student' section on your website.

This could include practical information (uniform, key dates, policies, transport information etc.), news (and a blog?) from current students, a countdown clock and even a forum for parents and students to ask questions of current students and parents.

4. Send them regular news updates.

Parents and students want to know what is happening in the school. You can create a specific newsletter for them, send them your current school newsletter or select and email a list of new stories from your website. Once a month as a good frequency for this.

5. Include them in existing events.

If you have musical, sporting, academic, religious or drama events invite parents who have shown an interest in these areas. Consider a special performance or session in an existing event such as an art exhibition for new parents.

6. Hold dedicated events.

Many schools have a day during the summer term for new students to attend. If you do this already, consider offering something for the parents as well as the students - if you don't offer this type of day, you should!

7. Act on any feedback.

Make sure that the school team dealing with new students meets regularly and answers queries and passes on concerns.

d) Managing Data – Customer Relationship Management

Once you have gathered information about potential customers you need to store this data so it can be used. While it may be possible to do this in a spreadsheet for a small school, it is likely that this information will be stored in a database. This can be done in a bespoke database (e.g. in Access), a contact system (Outlook), or a fully-fledged Customer Relationship Management programme such as those offered by salesforce.com.

Which system you use depends on your budget, the size of the data you need to hold and the complexity of the tasks you would like to use. At a minimum you need to be able to add further information about stakeholders and mail and e-mail merge documents. You might also want to schedule meetings, track telephone conversations and automate the tracking of advertising effectiveness.

The cost of these systems will range dramatically, but it is important to consider the additional time and costs of creating your own fields and of training key staff in their use. In addition, more complex systems offer cost savings in identifying the best places to put your advertising budget.

It is worth discussing this with the IT team at your school as there may well already be databases that track students that can be adapted to suit your needs. In particular private schools that use student-tracking systems such as Capita's SIMS[31] may find that this can be used as a CRM tool.

---

[31]capita-sims.co.uk

e) Great admissions IT on a shoestring

EXPERT ADVICE from marketingadviceforschools.com

By Tim Latham, schools marketing consultant

After many years in the commercial world, looking after marketing, sales and the technologies to support those functions, I've been interested to see how schools are addressing similar areas. Over the last year I've visited and started to help a range of independent schools. Various lessons have emerged about the IT systems to support admissions. Hopefully you will find my observations helpful - and please add your own!

Myth 1: Schools Are Different.

Well yes schools are different, most obviously in that you aren't overtly in the profit maximisation game. But that one issue aside all of my many commercial clients have been very different. Industries have grown to serve the education sector and to perpetuate the feeling that "schools are different" and therefore need different (more expensive) products & services. Be assured that all of the hundreds of thousands of businesses out there in the UK have a need to track their interactions with potential customers but they don't all feel the need to develop a customer relationship management (CRM) system bespoke for their sub-sector.

Myth 2: You Need a Bespoke Admissions System.

Years ago off the shelf CRM systems just did the basics, were essentially contact listings and many industries felt the need for their suppliers to develop bespoke solutions. These days the good CRM systems can be honed to fit very closely with almost every sector that I have come across.

Myth 3: Small is Beautiful.

How many clients or sites is the CRM system installed in? Bespoke industry solutions tend to count their user sites in tens or hundreds whereas the successful more generally applicable CRM systems have tens of thousands of users. More users means that the cost per user is dramatically reduced, the developer has more resources to keep the system abreast of industry latest standards, to continually improve usability and features. Small can be beautiful, but you normally pay for it. If you fully appreciate the costs of "going small" and make an informed decision that's fine, but many don't.

Myth 4: We Need It In-House On Our Server.

Do you like spending hundreds of pounds on servers, making sure they are constantly updated to the highest software and physical security standards, providing uninterruptible power supplies etc. - if so maybe you should be running an IT company? For the rest of us a "cloud hosted" service is dramatically less costly, more reliable, secure and accessible (with proper authorisation) from any web browser in any location. If the Head wants to see the state of play whilst on the train that's easily done with a cloud based service.

Here is my mini test to see whether your current admissions system is "up to the snuff":

1.	The telephone rings, it's Mrs Bloggs - can you get to her details on the system within 3 seconds?
2.	Mrs Bloggs again, you need to see a copy of the email she sent you three months ago. Can you get there in 3 seconds?
3.	Mrs Bloggs yet again, you need to access the report from her daughter's current Head, she sent it through some time ago. Can you get it in 3 seconds?

f) Personalised Newsletters

It is important to keep in touch with prospective parents and other stakeholders, especially as the decision to choose a school may take months or even years. Current parents are also important advocates and need to be kept aware of innovations and positive news stories from the school. A very useful tool for this is the newsletter or its modern equivalent the e-newsletter.

It is both polite and legally important to ask permission before sending emails to stakeholders. Sending written material does not require the same permission legally, but it is polite to have asked at an earlier stage of the process if you can send material.

A newsletter should contain news and information that reinforces the key messages. One tip is to make sure to ask the recipient to take action to keep in touch. Invitations to events, competitions and opportunities to network make the newsletter more interesting and more memorable.

Newsletters can be personalised by using mail-merge programmes. Mail-merging physical letters is a task that all schools do every day. Mail-merging e-mails is slightly more complex, although CRM programmes will often include this functionality and there are a wide number of commercial programmes that will automate the process - Marketing Advice for Schools uses Constant Contact[32] to manage its emailing for example.

Be careful not to send too much material, especially with email. 'Spamming' people with information they don't want can put them off. It is better to put a lot of material on your website or Twitter feed and then email once a month with a summary of information. Those who

---

[32] constantcontact.com

want more information regularly should be directed to subscribe to your Twitter or RSS feed.

g) How to create an excellent email newsletter

EXPERT ADVICE from marketingadviceforschools.com

By Sarah Clarke, Head of Marketing and Membership support at the Imperial Society of Teachers of Dancing

An email newsletter is an easy, instantaneous and relatively inexpensive way to grab the attention of your audience with relevant information that they want to read. Here are a few tips before you start!

Rule #1 – plan ahead

Too many people jump on the email newsletter, blog or Twitter bandwagon without fully thinking through why they might need these types of social media tools and how they can get the most out of them. Why are you starting an email newsletter? Do you want to better inform your current students about your classes, attract new students or give parents more information? And almost as important as who will be reading your email newsletter is who will be *writing* it. Even if you just send it out every other month it takes time to decide what you want to say, compile the information and maintain your email lists, so make sure you consider the resources required.

Rule #2 – do some research

There are lots of email marketing systems available which will allow you to design a simple template and include images, links and a "forward to a friend" button. Sign up to some other email newsletters and see what you think of them before you choose a system that works for you. You can always start off by creating a simple, text email which you can send from your own email account, but if you think you're going to keep building your list of email subscribers, it's often easier to have a separate "news" or "info" email address that the newsletter email comes from.

Rule #3 – ask permission

Spam accounts for approximately 78% of all email sent[1]. You don't want your message to go straight into someone's junk mail folder and with the vast amount of unwanted emails out there, it's even more important that your subscribers have willingly signed up. It's equally vital to be clear about expectations from the outset, which leads us to Rule #4…

Rule #4 – set expectations

Always set your subscribers' expectations during the opt-in process about what kinds of emails they'll be receiving. If you're starting a "newsletter" and that's what they've subscribed to, people will expect to read about your latest news when they open your email!

Rule #5 – think about your subject line

One of the jobs of an email newsletter is to grab attention quickly, so it's essential to create short, snappy and effective subject lines (how the email appears on the recipient's in-box). And the best subject lines are those that actually describe what's *in* the email. If your email is a newsletter, be clear and put the name and issue of the newsletter in your subject line. If your email is a special promotion, tell them right from the start (which is the subject line) what's inside.

For example, depending on the content, your subject line might feature an announcement about new classes, an upcoming event or a special offer. But be careful with your subject lines too – certain words like "free" tend to automatically send emails straight to spam folders.

Rule #6 – know your audience

An email newsletter can include any information you want it to. Part of planning ahead also includes thinking about who will be reading your email and what they want to see. Before embarking on a massive online marketing strategy, do an informal (or formal) poll among your students and parents to ask what information they would most like to see in an email. It might be upcoming competition dates, the latest results, links to photos on the website or just class times. Part of the beauty of an email newsletter is that you can change it easily, adding more content and linking to other online articles.

Rule #7 – stay relevant and interesting

The inherent creativity of the education world and the huge wealth of inspiring material you can generate will allow you to represent yourself online in a variety of engaging ways – from live streaming of performances to archived images. These can be included in your email newsletter as well. A clear, clean design with a template that you keep consistent each time will allow your audience to quickly scan and find the news that they're most interested in. For example, your diary dates could be set down one side with the main news in the middle, and a special offer at the bottom.

Rule #8 – be consistent

Email newsletters are a simple, fun, relevant – and consistent! – way of communicating with your students that they will look forward to seeing in their in-box. So make sure that you keep up regular contact and maintain your promise of weekly or monthly news. There's nothing more disappointing that signing up for something and then not receiving it!

Rule #9 – keep it simple

It's very easy to lose your audience with an email if they have to keep scrolling through reams of text. Keep it clear and concise and if you need to, link through to a longer article or message on your website. If you include a "call to action" or something that you want your subscribers to do, make it really obvious what they should do (click through to an online form, call to sign up for a class etc.) and make it clear why they should do it. Are they getting a discount, or is it a requirement for the new term?

Rule #10 – think of your ending

A short P.S. at the end of the emails can also catch attention and increase the number of people who click through to your website. Giving people an incentive to do something such as register for an event or read more information can often work well here.

Don't forget – all of the online communication tools that continue to pop up are just that, tools. Without a clear message and an audience to reach out to, they're like power drill without a wall and a picture to hang.

© ISTD Dance Examinations Board 2014

h) 'The least boring newsletter you are ever likely to read'

CASE STUDY from marketingadviceforschools.com

Thanks to Mark Squires of Langdale Priory School in Staffordshire who sent in his school's newsletter (below). As he pointed out, 'the content is driven by the children, as I hope you can tell'. The school website is also definitely worth a visit[33].

---

[33]langdaleprimary.co.uk

i) Networks

While the initial focus of marketing may be on recruitment of new students, it is important not to overlook the benefits of developing long term stakeholder networks – bringing together people with similar needs to create long lasting benefits. A school can offer the people in the network the chance to socialise and learn from each other and from other experts – in return the school can enhance its reputation and income. The network can also then be used to distribute marketing materials and messages to various communities. Three common networks are explored below, but innovative schools are constantly developing new ones – don't let this list limit you!

1. Parents

Nearly all schools have parent networks that allow current parents to meet, socialise and organise events to support the school. These can be very helpful to marketing professionals in schools and should be invited to take part in marketing activities. They can provide case studies, news stories and practical help in advertising the school and supporting events. They can also be part of the wider attraction of your school – for example your school may be able to put new parents moving into the area in touch with people from their faith or cultural background.

2. Former students

The next most common network to develop is alumni (former students). This is extremely common in the private sector, but many state schools are also seeing the benefits of this. The charity Future First[34], which has a goal to help schools harness the experiences and

---

[34] futurefirst.org.uk/in-schools/

skills of former students, sets out six benefits to a school of engaging alumni:

- Career and educational role models
- Mentors
- Work experience provision
- Volunteers (e.g. for reading clubs)
- Governors
- Potential donors

To start the process, former students can be offered reunions, newsletters and a networking website or Facebook page to help stay in touch with each other. Some schools also arrange sporting fixtures between former and current students.

3. Feeder Schools

Many secondary schools and sixth form colleges create networks of feeder schools, offering advice to teachers, special events for students and news of former students in return for the opportunity to publicise their school.

j) How to Build Networks for Your School

1. Be interested in your communities.

Ask your parents, teachers and alumni what they do outside of school and what they are interested in learning about. Find out about existing community groups in your area.

2. Act as a central community point.

A very easy action is to create an information station in your reception area for local community groups. Encourage parents to drop off flyers or posters for groups they are involved in. You could have a similar area on your website or use your social media platforms to pass on information. You can also do the same for teacher development in your staff room or Intranet.

3. Set up groups to fill gaps.

A lot of schools have had a great deal of success bringing parents into school to talk about parenting issues. Some arrange opportunities for fathers to meet up. Others will set up sporting clubs, link up parents from particular communities or those who have just moved into the area. You can arrange for teachers from different schools to meet up and train together, or help former students working in particular career areas to keep in touch.

4. Help groups by offering your space or facilities.

Schools may not be rich in cash terms but often have the best meeting facilities in the area. While the sports hall is often rented out, schools often forget that classrooms are empty in the evening or weekends. Don't forget other specialist rooms such as Art, Photography or ICT.

5. Give networks time and support.

It takes a while for groups to develop but once they exist you can use them to communicate positive messages about your school and engage community members in other activities that will help the school.

Chapter checklist...

- ☐ Are customer-facing staff aware of the importance of greeting stakeholders?
- ☐ Are systems and processes in place for gathering information about stakeholders?
- ☐ Do all relevant staff know how and when to use them?
- ☐ Are regular newsletters sent to interested stakeholders?
- ☐ Are events different from competitors and personalised?
- ☐ Is the school exploring ways of building networks of stakeholders for the long term?

CHAPTER NINE: MANAGING MARKETING (PART 2: REFLECTION)

a) Evaluating marketing

Implicit in much of the work of previous chapters is the need for regular reflection. One of the most famous quotations in marketing is from Lord Leverhulme, the founder of the giant Unilever consumer products business, who said, "I know half my advertising isn't working, I just don't know which half.[35]" Today's marketers put a lot of effort into reducing this waste and improving their marketing spend.

Using the strategic marketing plan described in Chapter 2 there are two distinct levels at which you can evaluate success.

1. Marketing objectives

Each activity should have a marketing objective (number of media articles achieved or applications received). Many of these are easy to track throughout the year, especially if effective CRM systems (discussed in chapter 8) have been used. Progress against these targets should be discussed at regular meetings involving all marketing staff.

If it appears that there are likely to be shortfalls against marketing targets, especially in recruitment of students, action needs to be taken. This could involve committing contingency funds to enhance successful activities, or reducing the focus on long-term marketing activity such as perceptions research to focus more on short-term activity such as contacting prospective parents personally.

Other ongoing activities should also be reviewed, even if overall targets are being met. For example, if a specific advert achieved very little interest you might decide not to use that advert again – although with

---

[35] http://en.wikipedia.org/wiki/William_Lever,_1st_Viscount_Leverhulme#Quotes

an established publication you would probably want to see a pattern over a few months before making too many changes. Conversely, if attending a local fair achieved a lot of interest a school might want to consider spending contingency money on similar events, or at least making a note to consider spending more money in this are next year.

Changes in perception are difficult to measure during the year in a cost-effective way. These are usually long-term changes and it is best to consider the first annual review as an opportunity to get interesting feedback for organisation and marketing planning and to refine future goals.

2. Organisational Objectives

The most useful way of showing the impact of marketing on your school (especially when meeting with your Business Manager or Bursar!) is to calculate the return on investment (ROI) by tracking which marketing activities directly led to new student recruitment.

Given that all schools now receive funding per student, you can project forward the income that student will bring to the school (usually over 5-7 years) and compare the income to the particular marketing activity and to the overall marketing spend. In a typical private school, each new student will bring in £50,000, while the figure may be closer to £20,000 in a state school.

Progress against other organisational objectives needs to be discussed regularly and the marketing function needs to attend the meetings where these are being discussed – usually at the SLT level. If organisational objectives change, marketing objectives should be changed to reflect them as soon as possible.

b) Improving the strategic marketing plan

Towards the end of the year, the organisation's objectives for the next year will be discussed. This will usually take place at Senior Management Team and Governor level. Marketing should be heavily involved in the process – informing the others in the process of changes in the wider market as well as reporting on changes in perceptions and the impact of marketing actions in the current year.

It is important that changes to organisational objectives are discussed and taken on board by marketing teams – it can be very easy to 'roll forward' current marketing activities without realising that they may not be appropriate – for example if a school has been building up numbers in their primary school but now wants to focus on secondary school, targeting nursery schools becomes less important.

If organisational objectives stay the same, marketers should come up with a new strategic marketing plan, using the same methods outlined in Chapter 2. However, the following information can now be used to improve the plan.

- Analysis of individual marketing activities from the previous year (which tactics worked best?)
- Analysis of recruitment data (in particular from where and from which schools did new students come from)
- New market research (including demographic changes and changes in the number, size and type of schools in the local area).
- New marketing innovations (are there new technologies, social media or processes that can be used to improve marketing or reduce costs?)

c) Keeping marketing going in the summer

Phew! We've made it... That's the reaction of most teachers and students at the end of the summer term.

But before we close up, we need to talk about marketing. It's easy to think that nothing happens in August, but for many parents the summer holiday itself is a key reminder that some important choices are coming up. Although they probably won't expect to be able to visit schools, they will want to do some research and have a detailed plan of action for the busy Autumn term.

What can schools do to engage and develop parents' interest over the summer? More and more schools have full-time marketing staff available for several weeks during the summer, but if not here are some tips...

1. Given that the number one source of information on a school is its website, make sure everything is up to date - don't wait until September to add details of the school's recruitment process (in many cases parents will be thinking two years ahead) or Open Days. Make sure you give visitors the chance to register their interest so you can contact them as soon as possible once staff return.

2. If the school office is going to be unmanned, make sure detailed voicemail and out-of-office emails are set up so that people know when the school can be contacted and how to find out key information in the meantime. Directing them to the website is a good idea.

3. Keep a presence on social media. A good idea is to repost the highlights of the last year on Facebook and Twitter using the scheduling features of programs such

as HootSuite[36] and TweetDeck[37] (I use the latter, but have heard good things about the former). I'd recommend posting the top 10 stories from the past year over a couple of weeks - a maximum of one story per day on Facebook, while on Twitter it's worth repeating each message two or three times a day. In the run-up to the A-level and GCSE exam result days you can change this to schedule specific reminders and advice for students.

4. Communicate great things that are happening in the summer. Two areas I've seen done really well are blogging stories about trips and giving updates on new building work. Both can be done by non-marketing staff (ask your caretaker to post pictures as a new building takes shape) and give a positive impression of the school.

5. Pre-book your Autumn advertising. Look at what worked well in previous years and make sure that you take advantage of early-booking discounts in the media that work for you. Wait until the exam results come out before confirming the artwork in order to put in some positive case studies and data.

---

[36] hootsuite.com

[37] https://about.twitter.com/products/tweetdeck

Chapter checklist...

- ☐ Are new leads tracked to identify the best ways of communicating?
- ☐ Are marketing targets reviewed against each marketing activity on a regular basis?
- ☐ Has the Return on Investment (ROI) been calculated for marketing in general and for individual marketing activities?
- ☐ Is there a plan for reviewing the overall marketing strategy on an annual or more regular basis?
- ☐ Is market research shared with SMT members and/or Governors who are developing the overall school strategy?

FURTHER READING

There are few specific resources for schools in the area of marketing (one reason for this book!) but there has been a lot written about marketing in general. The resources below provide an introduction to the key ideas and concepts expressed in this book.

Innovation in Marketing, Theodore Levitt, McGraw-Hill, 1962 (the book that moved marketing to centre stage in companies)

Marketing Management, Philip Kotler, Prentice Hall, 1996 (the most widely used marketing book in business schools – very strong on possible ways of meeting market needs)

Marketing Management and Strategy, Peter Doyle, Prentice Hall, 1998 (my MBA marketing textbook – very comprehensive and detailed)

Relationship Marketing: Creating Stakeholder Value, Christopher, Payne and Ballantyne, Butterworth Heinemann, 2002 (why relationships really matter in business)

Understanding Brands, Peter Cheverton, Kogan Page, 2006 (a highly readable introduction to what a brand really is)

The Non-Designer's Design Book, Robin Williams, Peachpit Press, 2008 (a great introduction to design if that's not your background)

Inbound Marketing – Get found using Google, Social Media and Blogs, Brian Halligan and Dharmesh Shah, John Wiley & Sons, 2010 (how can you use content to drive marketing?)

The New Rules of Marketing and PR, David Meerman Scott, John Wiley & Sons, 2011 (cutting edge ideas)

For the latest research into school marketing itself, visit the Library page of Marketing Advice for Schools. (marketingadviceforschools.com/library.html)

Made in the USA
Monee, IL
30 July 2021